LUCIA FÖRTHMANN

Cuddly Animals

TO CROCHET

28 Cute Toys to Make and Love

Includes an owl,
a fox, a whale and
other cuddly
animals

SEARCH PRESS

Introduction

Cuddly toys are something no child should be without! They accompany little people on dangerous, imaginary adventures, protect them against monsters in the night and are always on hand to comfort them.

These soft, cuddly animals are very special creatures with adorable features, just waiting for you to crochet them. So why not bring them to life in beautiful, bright colours and pass them on to an adoring youngster for lots of cuddles?

Made from high-quality yarns such as merino and organic cotton, they are wonderfully cosy and warming.

So what are you waiting for? Can you hear the sound of the hooves and paws of the approaching animals? But take care: these animals are addictive!

Happy crocheting,

Lucia Förthmann

Contents

Techniques

Magic ring

1.

Fold the yarn in a loop, with the yarn tail hanging down.

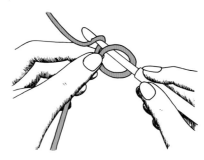

2.

Hold the loop firmly between your thumb and index finger, then insert the crochet hook through the loop, yarn over hook and draw through the loop.

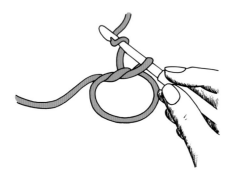

3.

Yarn over hook and draw through the loop again. This secures the ring.

4.

You can now crochet the stitches as usual. Always work into the ring, trapping the yarn tail as you go. When you have crocheted all your stitches, pull the yarn tail to close up the ring.

Single crochet (UK double crochet)

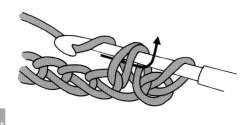

1.

Insert the hook into the next stitch, yarn over hook and draw through the yarn. There are now two loops on the hook.

2.

Yarn over again and pull it through both of the loops on the hook. This is the first single crochet (UK double crochet) stitch.

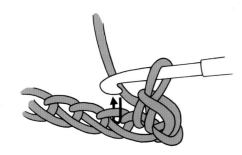

3.

Insert the hook into the next stitch and repeat steps 1 and 2.

Tulip stitch (t st)

Yarn over hook once, then insert the hook into the stitch, yarn over hook again and draw the yarn through. You now have three loops on the hook. Repeat this step twice more into the same stitch. You will have seven loops on the hook. Yarn over hook, then draw through all seven loops.

Half double crochet (UK half treble crochet)

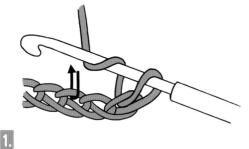

1.

Yarn over hook once, then insert the hook in the next stitch...

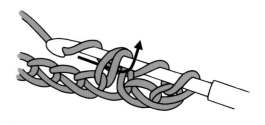

2.

...and draw the yarn through. There will be three loops on the hook.

3.

Yarn over hook and draw it through all three loops on the hook.

4.

This is what the finished half double crochet (UK half treble crochet) looks like.

Double crochet (UK treble crochet)

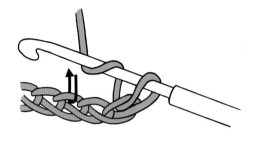

1.

Yarn over hook once, then insert the hook into the next stitch.

2.

Yarn over hook and draw through the stitch. There will be three loops on the hook.

3.

Yarn over hook again and draw through the first two loops on the hook. You will now have two loops left on the hook.

4.

Yarn over again and draw through the two remaining loops. The first double crochet (UK treble crochet) is complete.

Decreasing

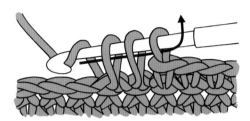

Stitches are decreased by working them together. Proceed as follows with single crochet (UK double crochet) stitches. Insert the hook through the next stitch as you would if crocheting a single crochet and draw the yarn through, but do not complete the stitch. Insert the hook into the next stitch and again draw the yarn through. You will have three loops on the hook. Yarn over hook, and draw through all three loops at the same time. The total number of stitches will have decreased by one.

Increasing

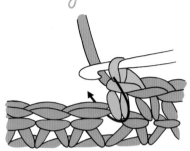

To double any kind of stitch, simply insert the hook into the same place the previous stitch was worked, and work the stitch as usual.

Mattress stitch

When finished, the mattress stitch cannot be seen on the right side. Place the two pieces of crocheted fabric side by side with the right side facing up. Insert the needle in the first and second stitches of the first row. Push the needle under two rows, then bring it back to the front between the first and second stitches of the row. Move to the opposite side, and feed the yarn under two rows. Repeat in a zigzag. Pull gently on the yarn at the end. This will close up the gap to create an invisible seam.

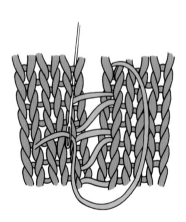

Raised stitch

Any kind of stitch can be worked as a raised stitch. These illustrations show a raised double crochet (UK treble crochet) from the front and the back.

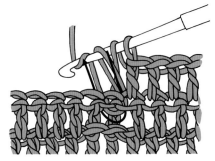

1. This shows a raised stitch from the back. Start the stitch as usual, then instead of inserting the hook through the two loops of the stitch, push it from back to front around the post of the stitch in the previous row. Draw the yarn through and complete the double crochet (UK treble crochet) as usual.

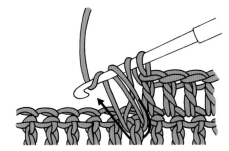

2. This shows a relief stitch from the front. Start the stitch as usual, then instead of inserting the hook through the two loops of the stitch, push it from front to back around the post of the stitch in the previous row. Draw the yarn through and complete the double crochet (UK treble crochet) as usual.

Whip stitch

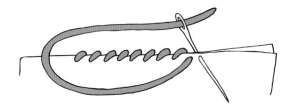

Use whip stitch and a tapestry needle to join the parts of your animal together. Place the two parts together with the right sides facing, or the front side to the inside. Secure the yarn, and draw the needle through both layers.

Continue working down the sides of the two parts, and secure the yarn neatly when you have finished.

French knot

Using a tapestry needle, bring the yarn up where you want your French knot. Wrap the yarn around the needle two or three times, and push it down again as close as possible to the same point. Tighten the yarn.

The size of the knot is determined by the number of times you wrap the thread around the needle.

Spike stitch

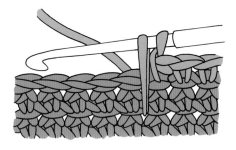

1.
Insert the hook between the stitches of the indicated row or round, yarn over and pull through.

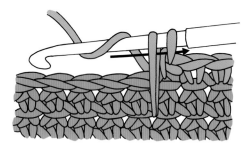

2.
You will now have two loops on the hook. Yarn over hook again, and pull through the two loops.

3.
The illustration shows a single crochet (UK double crochet) that was worked into the previous row, but you can use the same technique with any other stitch.

Bobble (MB)

Start as for a double crochet (UK treble crochet) stitch. Yarn over hook, then insert the hook in the stitch, and draw the yarn through the stitch. Yarn over hook again, and draw through the first two loops on the hook. There will be two loops left on the hook. Do not finish the double crochet (UK treble crochet) stitch. Work five more unfinished doubles (unfinished trebles) into the same stitch. There will be seven loops on the hook. Yarn over hook, and draw through all seven loops.

Colour changes in rows

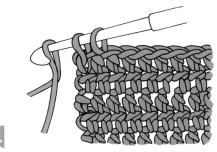

1.

Crochet your row to the end, until the last two loops are on the hook. Yarn over the new colour yarn...

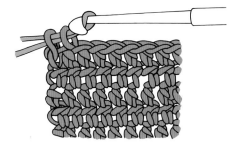

2.

... and draw the yarn through the last two loops of the final stitch.

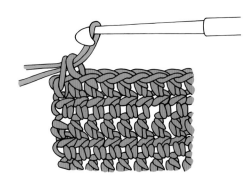

3.

Work the first turning chain for the next row in this new colour.

Abbreviations

beg = beginning
ch = chain(s)
col = colour(s)
dc = double crochet (UK tr/treble crochet)
dec = decrease
hdc = half double crochet (UK htr/half treble crochet)
inc = increase
MB = make bobble
rep = repeat
sc = single crochet (UK dc/double crochet)
sl st = slip stitch(es)
st(s) = stitch(es)
tog = together

Alternative yarn

If you cannot source the yarns stated in the patterns, you can use yarn of a similar weight and yardage to make the toys in this book.

FOREST

James
THE FOX

You can hear James playing beautiful music from a long way off. He lovingly refers to his flute as his best friend – without it, he is only half a fox. He is also the most fashionable animal in the forest, always wearing his boots and matching bow tie.

HEIGHT

★ Approx. 16½in (42cm)

MATERIALS

★ Lang Yarns Merino 120 (100% merino wool); 3 balls of Tangerine 0211, 1 ball each of Black 0004 and White 0001; 50g/131yd/120m
★ 2.5mm (B-1/UK 13) crochet hook
★ Toy stuffing
★ Tapestry needle

HEAD

Work in rounds. At the end of each round, work 1 sl st into first st in round, 1 ch and turn.

Round 1: using Tangerine yarn, work 6 sc (UK dc) into a magic ring (6 sts).

Round 2: inc 1 st three times, 3 sc (UK dc) (9 sts).

Round 3: *1 sc (UK dc), inc 1 st*, rep from * to * twice more, 3 sc (UK dc) (12 sts).

Round 4: 1 sc (UK dc) in each st of previous round (12 sts).

Round 5: 5 sc (UK dc), inc 1 st, 6 sc (UK dc) (13 sts).

Secure the yarn and fasten off.

Join Tangerine yarn to 4th st of previous round, and continue crocheting as follows:

Round 6: 2 sc (UK dc), inc 1 st twice, 2 sc (UK dc), change to White yarn, 1 sc (UK dc), inc 1 st, 3 sc (UK dc), inc 1 st, 1 sc (UK dc) (17 sts).

Round 7: 1 sc (UK dc), inc 1 st, 6 sc (UK dc), inc 1 st, 1 sc (UK dc), change to Tangerine yarn, 3 sc (UK dc), inc 1 st, 3 sc (UK dc) (20 sts).

Work rounds 8–13 as rows. Do not crochet a sl st into the first st of the round, instead turn work and ch 1. Sew up the resulting opening neatly at the end.

Row 8: 3 sc (UK dc), inc 1 st, 4 sc (UK dc), change to White yarn, inc 1 st,

10 sc (UK dc), inc 1 st (23 sts).

Row 9: inc 1 st, 2 sc (UK dc), inc 1 st, 6 sc (UK dc), inc 1 st, 2 sc (UK dc), inc 1 st, change to Tangerine yarn, inc 1 st, 3 sc (UK dc), inc 1 st, 3 sc (UK dc), inc 1 st (30 sts).

Row 10: inc 1 st, 4 sc (UK dc), inc 1 st twice, 4 sc (UK dc), inc 1 st, change to White yarn, 1 sc (UK dc), inc 1 st, 2 sc (UK dc), inc 1 st, 8 sc (UK dc), inc 1 st, 2 sc (UK dc), inc 1 st, 1 sc (UK dc) (38 sts).

Row 11: 22 sc (UK dc), change to Tangerine yarn, 16 sc (UK dc) (38 sts).

Row 12: inc 1 st, 6 sc (UK dc), inc 1 st, 6 sc (UK dc), inc 1 st, change to White yarn, 5 sc (UK dc), inc 1 st, 10 sc (UK dc), inc 1 st, 5 sc (UK dc) (44 sts).

Row 13: 24 sc (UK dc), change to Tangerine yarn, 20 sc (UK dc) (44 sts).

Fasten off White yarn. Continue working in rounds.

Round 14: inc 1 st, 3 sc (UK dc), inc 1 st, 3 sc (UK dc), inc 1 st, 2 sc (UK dc), inc 1 st, 3 sc (UK dc), inc 1 st, 3 sc (UK dc), inc 1 st, 24 sc (UK dc) (50 sts).

Round 15: 27 sc (UK dc), inc 1 st, *3 sc (UK dc), inc 1 st*, rep from * to * four more times, 2 sc (UK dc) (56 sts).

Rounds 16 and 17: 1 sc (UK dc) in each st of previous round (56 sts).

Round 18: 2 sc (UK dc), inc 1 st, *4 sc (UK dc), inc 1 st*, rep from * to * four more times, 28 sc (UK dc) (62 sts).

Rounds 19–22: 1 sc (UK dc) in each st of previous round (62 sts).

Using mattress stitch and Tangerine yarn, sew up the gap in the fox's face. This will create a neater transition than if you had completed the colour change in the relevant rows with 1 sl st in the first st.

Round 23: 37 sc (UK dc), inc 1 st, 14 sc (UK dc), inc 1 st, 9 sc (UK dc) (64 sts).

Rounds 24–28: 1 sc (UK dc) in each st of the previous round (64 sts).

Round 29: 42 sc (UK dc), dec 1 st, *3 sc (UK dc), dec 1 st*, rep from * to * twice more, 5 sc (UK dc) (60 sts).

Round 30: *8 sc (UK dc), dec 1 st*, rep from * to * five more times (54 sts).

Round 31: *7 sc (UK dc), dec 1 st*, rep from * to * five more times (48 sts).

Round 32: *6 sc (UK dc), dec 1 st*, rep from * to * five more times (42 sts).

Stuff the head.

Round 33: *5 sc (UK dc), dec 1 st*, rep from * to * five more times (36 sts).

Round 34: *4 sc (UK dc), dec 1 st*, rep from * to * five more times (30 sts).

Round 35: *3 sc (UK dc), dec 1 st*, rep from * to * five more times (24 sts).

Round 36: *2 sc (UK dc), dec 1 st*, rep from * to * five more times (18 sts).

Round 37: *1 sc (UK dc), dec 1 st*, rep from * to * five more times (12 sts).

Round 38: dec 1 st six times (6 sts).

Round 39: *skip 1 st, 1 sl st*, rep from * to * twice more (3 sts).

Secure the yarn and fasten off.

BODY

Work in rounds. At the end of each round, work 1 sl st into first st in round, 1 ch and turn.

Round 1: using Tangerine yarn, work 6 sc (UK dc) into a magic ring (6 sts).

Round 2: inc 1 st six times (12 sts).

Round 3: *1 sc (UK dc), inc 1 st*, rep from * to * five more times (18 sts).

Round 4: *2 sc (UK dc), inc 1 st*, rep from * to * five more times (24 sts).

Round 5: *3 sc (UK dc), inc 1 st*, rep from * to * five more times (30 sts).

Round 6: *4 sc (UK dc), inc 1 st*, rep from * to * five more times (36 sts).

Round 7: *5 sc (UK dc), inc 1 st*, rep from * to * five more times (42 sts).

Round 8: *6 sc (UK dc), inc 1 st*, rep from * to * five more times (48 sts).

Round 9: *7 sc (UK dc), inc 1 st*, rep from * to * five more times (54 sts).

Round 10: *8 sc (UK dc), inc 1 st*, rep from * to * five more times (60 sts).

Rounds 11–30: 1 sc (UK dc) in each st of the previous round (60 sts).

Round 31: *8 sc (UK dc), dec 1 st*, rep from * to * five more times (54 sts).

Rounds 32–40: 1 sc (UK dc) in each st of the previous round (60 sts).

Round 41: *7 sc (UK dc), dec 1 st*, rep from * to * five more times (48 sts).

Rounds 42–46: 1 sc (UK dc) in each st of the previous round (48 sts).

Round 47: *6 sc (UK dc), dec 1 st*, rep from * to * five more times (42 sts).

Rounds 48–50: 1 sc (UK dc) in each st of the previous round (42 sts).

Stuff the body.

Round 51: *5 sc (UK dc), dec 1 st*, rep from * to * five more times (36 sts).

Round 52: *4 sc (UK dc), dec 1 st*, rep from * to * five more times (30 sts).

Round 53: *3 sc (UK dc), dec 1 st*, rep from * to * five more times (24 sts).

Round 54: *2 sc (UK dc), dec 1 st*, rep from * to * five more times (18 sts).

Round 55: *1 sc (UK dc), dec 1 st*, rep from * to * five more times (12 sts).

Round 56: dec 1 st six times (6 sts).

Round 57: *skip 1 st, 1 sl st*, rep from * to * twice more (3 sts).

Secure the yarn and fasten off.

COLLAR

Work in rows. At the end of each row, work 1 ch and turn.

Row 1: using White yarn, work 13 ch, 1 sc (UK dc) into second ch from hook, 1 sc (UK dc) into the remaining 11 ch (12 sts).

Row 2: 1 sc (UK dc) in each st of previous row (12 sts).

Row 3: 4 sc (UK dc), dec 1 st twice, 4 sc (UK dc) (10 sts).

Rows 4–6: 1 sc (UK dc) in each st of previous row (10 sts).

Row 7: 3 sc (UK dc), dec 1 st twice, 3 sc (UK dc) (8 sts).

Rows 8–10: 1 sc (UK dc) in each st of previous row (8 sts).

Row 11: 2 sc (UK dc), dec 1 st twice, 2 sc (UK dc) (6 sts).

Row 12: dec 1 st, 2 sc (UK dc), dec 1 st (4 sts).

Row 13: dec 1 st twice (2 sts).

Row 14: dec 1 st (1 st).

Row 15: 1 sc (UK dc) (1 st).

Secure the yarn and fasten off, leaving a long tail.

BOW TIE

Work in rows. At the end of each row, work 1 ch and turn.

Row 1: using Black yarn, work 5 ch, 1 sc (UK dc) into second ch from hook, 1 sc (UK dc) into the remaining 3 ch (4 sts).

Row 2: 1 sc (UK dc) into each st of previous row (4 sts).

Row 3: dec 1 st twice (2 sts).

Rows 4 and 5: 1 sc (UK dc) into each st of previous row (2 sts).

Row 6: inc 1 st twice (4 st).

Rows 7 and 8: 1 sc (UK dc) into each st of previous row (4 sts).

Secure the yarn and fasten off. Wind Black yarn repeatedly around rows 4 and 5 of the bow tie and secure with a knot.

EARS (MAKE 2 TANGERINE AND BLACK, 2 WHITE)

Work in rows. At the end of each row, work 1 ch and turn.

Row 1: using Tangerine yarn, work 10 ch, 1 sc (UK dc) into second ch from hook, 1 sc (UK dc) into the remaining 8 ch (9 sts).

Row 2: 1 sc (UK dc) into each st of previous row (9 sts).

Row 3: dec 1 st, 5 sc (UK dc), dec 1 st (7 sts).

Row 4: 1 sc (UK dc) into each st of previous row (7 sts).

Change to Black yarn.

Row 5: 1 sc (UK dc) into each st of previous row (7 sts).

Row 6: dec 1 st, 3 sc (UK dc), dec 1 st (5 sts).

Rows 7 and 8: 1 sc (UK dc) into each st of previous row (5 sts).

Row 9: dec 1 st, 1 sc (UK dc), dec 1 st (3 sts).

Rows 10 and 11: 1 sc (UK dc) into each st of previous row (3 sts).

Row 12: 3 sc (UK dc) tog (1 st).

Secure the yarn and fasten off. Work a second ear as above, and two more ears in White yarn. Place one white ear and one tangerine and black yarn together and join evenly using sc (UK dc) along the edges. Have the white ear in front of you, and work in Tangerine or Black yarn as appropriate.

TIP OF SHOE (MAKE 2)

Work in rounds. At the end of each round, work 1 sl st into first st in round, 1 ch and turn.

Round 1: using Black yarn, work 3 sc (UK dc) into a magic ring (3 sts).

Round 2: inc 1 st three times (6 sts).

Round 3: *1 sc (UK dc), inc 1 st*, rep from * to * twice more (9 sts).

Round 4: *2 sc (UK dc), inc 1 st*, rep from * to * twice more (12 sts).

Rounds 5–7: 1 sc (UK dc) in each st of previous round (12 sts).

Change to White yarn.

Round 8: 5 sc (UK dc), inc 1 st twice, 5 sc (UK dc) (14 sts).

Round 9: 6 sc (UK dc), inc 1 st, 2 sc (UK dc), inc 1 st, 4 sc (UK dc) (16 sts).

Round 10: 7 sc (UK dc), inc 1 st twice, 7 sc (UK dc) (18 sts).

Round 11: 1 sc (UK dc) into each st of previous round (18 sts).

Secure the yarn and fasten off.

LEGS (MAKE 2)

Start off working in rounds. At the end of each round work 1 sl st in the first st of the round and ch 1. Do not turn.

Tip: For this pattern, the colours frequently change within a round. Crochet around the yarn not currently being used.

Round 1: using Black yarn, work 6 sc (UK dc) into a magic ring (6 sts).

Round 2: inc 1 st six times (12 sts).

Rounds 3 and 4: 1 sc (UK dc) into each st of previous round (12 sts).

Round 5: 4 sc (UK dc) in Black yarn, 4 sc (UK dc) in White yarn, 4 sc (UK dc) in Black yarn (12 sts).

Round 6: 3 sc (UK dc) in Black yarn, 6 sc (UK dc) in White yarn, 3 sc (UK dc) in Black yarn (12 sts).

Round 7: 2 sc (UK dc) in Black yarn, 8 sc (UK dc) in White yarn, 2 sc (UK dc) in Black yarn (12 sts).

Round 8: 1 sc (UK dc) in Black yarn, 10 sc (UK dc) in White yarn, 1 sc (UK dc) in Black yarn (12 sts).

Change to White yarn.

Round 9: 1 sc (UK dc) into each st of previous round (12 sts).

Continue working in rounds, but turn at the end of each round.

Rounds 10–16: 1 sc (UK dc) into each st of previous row (12 sts).

Change to Tangerine yarn.

Round 17: work into the back bar of the stitch only: 1 sc (UK dc) into each st of previous row (12 sts).

Rounds 18–28: 1 sc (UK dc) into each st of previous row (12 sts).

Round 29: inc 1 st 12 times (24 sts).

Rounds 30–33: 1 sc (UK dc) into each st of previous row (24 sts).

Secure the yarn and fasten off. Stuff the leg.

ARMS (MAKE 2)

Work in rounds. At the end of each round, work 1 sl st into first st in row, 1 ch and turn.

Round 1: using Black yarn, work 6 sc (UK dc) into a magic ring (6 sts).

Round 2: inc 1 st six times (12 sts).

Rounds 3–12: 1 sc (UK dc) into each st of previous round (12 sts).

Change to Tangerine yarn.

Rounds 13–16: 1 sc (UK dc) into each st of previous round (12 sts).

Round 17: dec 1 st twice, inc 1 st four times, dec 1 st twice (12 sts).

Round 18: 1 sc (UK dc) into each st of previous row (12 sts).

Round 19: dec 1 st twice, inc 1 st four times, dec 1 st twice (12 sts).

Round 20: 1 sc (UK dc) into each st of previous round (12 sts).

Round 21: dec 1 st twice, inc 1 st four times, dec 1 st twice (12 sts).

Rounds 22–34: 1 sc (UK dc) into each st of previous round (12 sts).

Secure the yarn and fasten off. Stuff the arm.

TAIL

Work in rounds. At the end of each round, work 1 sl st into first st in round, 1 ch and turn.

Round 1: using White yarn, work 3 sc (UK dc) into a magic ring (3 sts).

Round 2: inc 1 st three times (6 sts)

Round 3: *1 sc (UK dc), inc 1 st*, rep from * to * twice more (9 sts).

Round 4: *2 sc (UK dc), inc 1 st*, rep from * to * twice more (12 sts).

Round 5: *3 sc (UK dc), inc 1 st*, rep from * to * twice more (15 sts).

Round 6: *4 sc (UK dc), inc 1 st*, rep from * to * twice more (18 sts).

Round 7: *5 sc (UK dc), inc 1 st*, rep from * to * twice more (21 sts).

Round 8: *6 sc (UK dc), inc 1 st*, rep from * to * twice more (24 sts).

Round 9: *7 sc (UK dc), inc 1 st*, rep from * to * twice more (27 sts).

Round 10: *8 sc (UK dc), inc 1 st*, rep from * to * twice more (30 sts).

Round 11: *9 sc (UK dc), inc 1 st*, rep from * to * twice more (33 sts).

Round 12: *10 sc (UK dc), inc 1 st*, rep from * to * twice more (36 sts).

Rounds 13–18: 1 sc (UK dc) into each st of previous round (36 sts).

Round 19: *10 sc (UK dc), dec 1 st*, rep from * to * twice more (33 sts).

Round 20: 1 sc (UK dc) into each st of previous round (33 sts).

Round 21: *9 sc (UK dc), dec 1 st*, rep from * to * twice more (30 sts).

Round 22: 1 sc (UK dc) into each st of previous round (30 sts).

Round 23: *work 1 sc (UK dc) in White yarn, then 1 sc (UK dc) in Tangerine yarn*, rep from * to * to end (30 sts). Change to Tangerine yarn.

Round 24: 1 sc (UK dc) into each st of previous round (30 sts).

Round 25: *8 sc (UK dc), dec 1 st*, rep from * to * twice more (27 sts).

Round 26: 1 sc (UK dc) into each st of previous round (27 sts). Stuff the tail.

Round 27: *7 sc (UK dc), dec 1 st*, rep from * to * twice more (24 sts).

Rounds 28 and 29: 1 sc (UK dc) into each st of previous round (24 sts).

Round 30: *6 sc (UK dc), dec 1 st*, rep from * to * twice more (21 sts).

Round 31: 1 sc (UK dc) into each st of previous round (21 sts).

Round 32: *5 sc (UK dc), dec 1 st*, rep from * to * twice more (18 sts).

Round 33: 1 sc (UK dc) into each st of previous round (18 sts).

Round 34: *4 sc (UK dc), dec 1 st*, rep from * to * twice more (15 sts).

Rounds 35–48: 1 sc (UK dc) into each st of previous round (15 sts).

Secure the yarn and fasten off. Stuff the remainder of the fox's tail.

EYES (MAKE 2)

Round 1: using Black yarn, work 6 sc (UK dc) into a magic ring (6 sts).

Sl st into the first st. Secure the yarn and fasten off.

FINISHING OFF

Sew the eyes to the front of the head, seven rounds above the nose, and embroider two French knots onto each eye using White yarn. Sew two eyelashes in Black yarn beside each eye. Attach an ear to each side of the head using whip stitch. Attach the last round of the body to the underside of the head using mattress stitch. Sew the collar to the body just below the head, with the first row towards the head. Sew the bow tie in the middle of rows 1–3 of the collar. For each arm, press the last rounds together, and attach the edges to the body using whip stitch. Sew the last round of the tip of the shoe to the bottom of the leg, where the white area widens with each round. Stuff the tip of the shoe before sewing the last stitches together. Sew the last round of each leg to the underside of the body using whip stitch, with the tips of the shoes pointing forwards. Embroider three French knots to the outsides of each boot using Black yarn. Press the last round of the tail together and sew to the back of the body using whip stitch.

Luna
THE OWL

Too-whit, too-whoooo!
This lady just loves singing all
night long! Up in her cosy
nest, there's nothing she loves
more than listening to opera
arias, and having a little go
along with the sopranos.

HEIGHT
★ Approx. 8½in (22cm)

MATERIALS
★ Lang Yarns Merino 120 (100% merino wool); 1 ball each of Dark Brown Mélange 0368, Beige Mélange 0226, Dark Beige Mélange 0326 and White 0001, and scraps of Tangerine 0211 and Black 0004; 50g/131yd/120m
★ 2.5mm (B-1/UK 13) crochet hook
★ Toy stuffing
★ Tapestry needle

BODY
Work in spiral rounds. This means the rounds are not finished with a sl st, nor do you work a turning ch at the beg of a new round.

Round 1: using Beige Mélange yarn, work 6 sc (UK dc) into a magic ring (6 sts).

Round 2: inc 1 st six times (12 sts).

Round 3: *1 sc (UK dc), inc 1 st*, rep from * to * five more times (18 sts).

Round 4: *2 sc (UK dc), inc 1 st*, rep from * to * five more times (24 sts).

Round 5: *3 sc (UK dc), inc 1 st*, rep from * to * five more times (30 sts).

Round 6: *4 sc (UK dc), inc 1 st*, rep from * to * five more times (36 sts).

Round 7: *5 sc (UK dc), inc 1 st*, rep from * to * five more times (42 sts).

Round 8: *6 sc (UK dc), inc 1 st*, rep from * to * five more times (48 sts).

Round 9: *7 sc (UK dc), inc 1 st*, rep from * to * five more times (54 sts).

Round 10: 1 sc (UK dc) into each st of previous round (54 sts).

Round 11: *8 sc (UK dc), inc 1 st*, rep from * to * five more times (60 sts).

Round 12: 1 sc (UK dc) into each st of previous round (60 sts).

Round 13: *9 sc (UK dc), inc 1 st*, rep from * to * five more times (66 sts).

Round 14: 1 sc (UK dc) into each st of previous round (66 sts).

Round 15: *10 sc (UK dc), inc 1 st*, rep from * to * five more times (72 sts).

Round 16: 1 sc (UK dc) into each st of previous round (72 sts).

Rounds 17–23: 1 sc (UK dc) into each st of previous round (72 sts).

Round 24: *10 sc (UK dc), dec 1 st*, rep from * to * five more times (66 sts).

Round 25: *9 sc (UK dc), dec 1 st*, rep from * to * five more times (60 sts).

Round 26: *8 sc (UK dc), dec 1 st*, rep from * to * five more times (54 sts).

Round 27: work into the front bar of the stitch only: *[1 sc (UK dc) and 1 hdc (UK htr)] in 1 st, 3 sc (UK dc) in 1 st, [1 hdc (UK htr) and 1 sc (UK dc)] in 1 st*, rep from * to * seventeen more times.

Secure the yarn and fasten off. Join Dark Beige Mélange yarn to the back bar of the first st in round 26 and continue crocheting as follows:

Round 28: 1 sc (UK dc) into each st of previous round (54 sts).

Round 29: *2 sc (UK dc), 1 spike sc (UK dc) into round 26*, rep from * to * seventeen more times, sl st to first sc (UK dc) of round (54 sts).

Round 30: work into the front bar of the stitch only: *[1 hdc (UK htr) and 1 sc (UK dc)] in 1 st, [1 sc (UK dc) and 1 hdc (UK htr)] in 1 st, 3 dc (UK tr) in 1 st*, rep from * to * seventeen more times.

Secure the yarn and fasten off. Join Dark Brown Mélange yarn to the back bar of the first st of round 29, and continue crocheting as follows.

Round 31: 1 sc (UK dc) into each st of previous round (54 sts).

Round 32: *1 spike sc (UK dc) into round 29, 2 sc (UK dc)*, rep from * to * seventeen more times (54 sts).

Round 33: work into the front bar of the stitch only: *3 dc (UK tr) in 1 st, [1 hdc (UK htr) and 1 sc (UK dc)] in 1 st, [1 sc (UK dc) and 1 hdc (UK htr)] in 1 st*, rep from * to * seventeen more times.

Secure the yarn and fasten off. Join Beige Mélange yarn to the back bar of the first st of round 32, and continue crocheting as follows:

Round 34: 1 sc (UK dc) into each st of previous round (54 sts).

Round 35: *1 sc (UK dc), 1 spike sc (UK dc) into round 32, 1 sc (UK dc)*, rep from * to * seventeen more times (54 sts).

Round 36: 1 sc (UK dc) into each st of previous round (54 st).

Change to Dark Brown Mélange yarn.

Round 37: 1 hdc (UK htr) into each st of previous round (54 sts).

Change to Beige Mélange yarn.

Round 38: *2 sc (UK dc), 1 spike sc (UK dc) into previous round*, rep from * to * seventeen more times (54 sts).

Round 39: 1 hdc (UK htr) into each st of previous round (54 sts).

Change to Dark Brown Mélange yarn.

Rounds 40–53: rep rounds 38 and 39, changing to Beige Mélange or Dark Brown Mélange yarn after every 2 rounds (54 sts).

Change to Beige Mélange yarn.

Round 54: *2 sc (UK dc), 1 spike sc (UK dc) into previous round*, rep from * to * seventeen more times (54 sts).

Round 55: *7 sc (UK dc), dec 1 st*, rep from * to * five more times (48 sts).

Change to Dark Beige Mélange yarn.

Round 56: work into the back bar of the stitch only: *6 sc (UK dc), dec 1 st*, rep from * to * five more times (42 sts). Stuff the body.

Round 57: *5 sc (UK dc), dec 1 st*, rep from * to * five more times (36 sts).

Round 58: *4 sc (UK dc), dec 1 st*, rep from * to * five more times (30 sts).

Round 59: *3 sc (UK dc), dec 1 st*, rep from * to * five more times (24 sts).

Round 60: *2 sc (UK dc), dec 1 st*, rep from * to * five more times (18 sts).

Round 61: *1 sc (UK dc), dec 1 st*, rep from * to * five more times (12 sts).

Round 62: dec 1 st six times (6 sts).

Round 63: *skip 1 st, 1 sl st*, rep from * to * twice more (3 sts).

Secure the yarn and fasten off.

WINGS (MAKE 2 DARK BROWN, 2 DARK BEIGE)

Work in spiral rounds. This means the rounds are not finished with a sl st, nor do you work a turning ch at the beg of a new round.

Round 1: work 16 ch, 1 sc (UK dc) in second ch from hook, 1 sc (UK dc) into next 13 ch, 3 sc (UK dc) into last ch. Continue working on the other side of the length of ch: 13 sc (UK dc), 2 sc (UK dc) into ch with first st (32 sts).

Round 2: inc 1 st, 2 sc (UK dc), 2 hdc (UK htr), 8 dc (UK tr), work 2 dc (UK tr) into 1 st five times, 8 dc (UK tr), 2 hdc (UK htr), 2 sc (UK dc), inc 1 st, 1 sc (UK dc) (39 sts).

Round 3: 1 sc (UK dc), inc 1 st, 2 sc (UK dc), 2 hdc (UK htr), 8 dc (UK tr), work 2 dc (UK tr) into 1 st ten times, 8 dc (UK tr), 2 hdc (UK htr), 5 sc (UK dc) (50 sts).

Round 4: 1 tulip st, 1 sc (UK dc), 1 ch. Do not work the remainder of the st.

Secure the yarn and fasten off. Place one wing in Dark Brown Mélange yarn and one in Dark Beige Mélange yarn together and sew them together along the last round using Dark Beige Mélange yarn. Stuff the wing before sewing up the last few stitches.

RIGHT EYE

Round 1: using White yarn, work 6 sc (UK dc) into a magic ring (6 sts). Sl st into first st. Do not turn the work.

Round 2: inc 1 st five times, leave 1 st unworked (10 sts). Do not work sl st into first st, 1 ch and turn.

Round 3: *1 sc (UK dc), inc 1 st*, rep from * to * twice more, 2 sc (UK dc), inc 1 st, 1 sc (UK dc) (14 sts). Do not work sl st into first st, 1 ch and turn.

Round 4: 2 sc (UK dc), [1 hdc (UK htr) and 1 dc (UK tr)] into 1 st, *1 dc (UK tr), 2 sc (UK dc) into 1 st*, rep from * to * three more times, 3 dc (UK tr). Do not turn the work, but continue crocheting along the side of the dc (UK tr): 2 sc (UK dc) into the side of the dc (UK tr), continue working sc (UK dc) evenly along the edge to the first st of the round.

Secure the yarn and fasten off.

LEFT EYE

Work as for rounds 1 and 2 for the right eye, then continue as follows:

Round 3: 1 sc (UK dc), inc 1 st, 2 sc (UK dc), *inc 1 st, 1 sc (UK dc)*, rep from * to * twice more (14 sts). Do not work sl st into first st, 1 ch and turn work.

Round 4: 3 dc (UK tr), *2 dc (UK tr) in 1 st, 1 dc (UK tr)*, rep from * to * 3 more times, [1 dc (UK tr) and 1 hdc (UK htr)] in 1 st, 2 sc (UK dc). Do not turn the

FINISHING OFF

Sew the rounded side of each wing to the sides of the body. Using whip stitch, sew one of each colour ear to each side of the top of the head.

Position the eyes together with the straight sides facing, and attach to the head using backstitch, working 2 st from the last round of the eye. Attach Dark Brown Mélange yarn to the bottom edge of the right eye and work 1 round sc (UK dc) along the edge. Work a few sc (UK dc) between the eyes on the head to form a 'V', then continue crocheting along the edge of the left eye and back to where you started. Sl st into first st of the round. Sew a pupil just below the middle of each eye and add two French knots in White yarn to each pupil. Sew two eyelashes in Black yarn beside each eye. Finally, sew the beak between the eyes with the tip facing down.

work, but continue working along the side of the last sc (UK dc), then work evenly along the edge to the first st of the round.

Secure the yarn and fasten off.

PUPIL

Round 1: using Black yarn, work 6 sc (UK dc) into a magic ring (6 sts). Join in the round with 1 sl st into the first st. Change to Tangerine yarn.

Round 2: work into the back bar of the stitch only: inc 1 sc (UK dc) six times (12 sts). Secure the yarn and fasten off.

BEAK

Work in spiral rounds. This means the rounds are not finished with a sl st, nor do you work a turning ch at the beg of a new round.

Round 1: using Dark Beige Mélange yarn, work 9 ch, join in a round with 1 sl st into first ch, 1 sc (UK dc) into each ch (9 sts).

Round 2: 1 sc (UK dc) into each st of previous round (9 sts).

Round 3: dec 1 st, 7 sc (UK dc) (8 sts).

Round 4: 1 sc (UK dc), dec 1 st, 5 sc (UK dc) (7 sts).

Round 5: 2 sc (UK dc), dec 1 st, 4 sc (UK dc) (6 sts).

Round 6: dec 1 st, 4 sc (UK dc) (5 sts).

Round 7: dec 1 st twice, skip 1 st (2 sts). Secure the yarn and fasten off.

EARS (MAKE 2 BEIGE, 2 DARK BROWN)

Work 8 ch, 1 sc (UK dc) into second ch from hook, 2 sc (UK dc), 2 hdc (UK htr), 2 dc (UK tr), 1 ch, and turn. Now work 1 round sc (UK dc) around this piece. Secure the yarn and fasten off.

Rosie
THE DEER

Rosie is - and loves! - a sweetie! She loves nothing more than wallowing in lollipops and sweet treats.

HEIGHT
★ Approx. 12½in (32cm)

MATERIALS
★ Austermann Merino 160 (100% merino wool); 1 ball each of Lollipop 256, Natur 210 and Pink Lipstick 241, and scraps of Brombeer 220, White 201 and Black 202; 50g/174yd/160m
★ 2.5mm (B-1/UK 13) crochet hook
★ Toy stuffing
★ Tapestry needle

Note: In this pattern, the colours often change within a round or row. Crochet around yarn not currently being used.

HEAD
Work in rounds. At the end of each row, work 1 sl st into first st in round, 1 ch and turn.

Round 1: using Natur yarn, work 6 sc (UK dc) into a magic ring (6 sts).

Round 2: inc 1 st twice in Natur yarn, inc 2 st twice in Lollipop yarn, inc 1 st twice in Natur yarn (12 sts).

Round 3: 4 sc (UK dc) in Natur yarn, 4 sc (UK dc) in Lollipop yarn, 4 sc (UK dc) in Natur yarn (12 sts).

Round 4: *1 sc (UK dc), inc 1 st*, rep from * to * once more, 1 sc (UK dc) in Natur yarn, inc 1 st, 1 sc (UK dc), inc 1 st in Lollipop yarn, *1 sc (UK dc), inc 1 st*, rep from * to * once more in Natur yarn (18 sts).

Round 5: 7 sc (UK dc) in Natur yarn, 5 sc (UK dc) in Lollipop yarn, 6 sc (UK dc) in Natur yarn (18 sts).

Round 6: *2 sc (UK dc), inc 1 st*, rep from * to * once more, 1 sc (UK dc) in Natur yarn, 1 sc (UK dc), inc 1 st, 2 sc (UK dc), inc 1 st in Lollipop yarn, *2 sc (UK dc), inc 1 st*, rep from * to * once more in Natur yarn (24 sts).

Round 7: *3 sc (UK dc), inc 1 st*, rep from * to * once more, 1 sc (UK dc) in Natur yarn, 2 sc (UK dc), inc 1 st, 3 sc (UK dc), inc 1 st in Lollipop yarn, *3 sc (UK dc), inc 1 st*, rep from * to * once more in Natur yarn (30 sts).

Round 8: *4 sc (UK dc), inc 1 st*, rep from * to * once more, 1 sc (UK dc) in Natur yarn, 3 sc (UK dc), inc 1 st, 4 sc (UK dc), inc 1 st in Lollipop yarn, *4 sc (UK dc), inc 1 st*, rep from * to * once more in Natur yarn (36 sts).

Round 9: 14 sc (UK dc) in Natur yarn, 10 sc (UK dc) in Lollipop yarn, 12 sc (UK dc) in Natur yarn (36 sts).

Round 10: *5 sc (UK dc), inc 1 st*, rep from * to * once more, 1 sc (UK dc), inc 1 st in Natur yarn, 10 sc (UK dc) in Lollipop yarn, inc 1 st, 4 sc (UK dc), inc 1 st, 5 sc (UK dc), inc 1 st in Natur yarn (42 sts).

Round 11: 16 sc (UK dc), inc 1 st in Natur yarn, 10 sc (UK dc) in Lollipop yarn, inc 1 st, 14 sc (UK dc) in Natur yarn (44 sts).

Round 12: *6 sc (UK dc), inc 1 st*, rep from * to * once more, 4 sc (UK dc) in Natur yarn, 10 sc (UK dc) in Lollipop yarn, 8 sc (UK dc), inc 1 st, 6 sc (UK dc), inc 1 st in Natur yarn (48 sts).

Round 13: 20 sc (UK dc) in Natur yarn, inc 1 st, 8 sc (UK dc), inc 1 st in Lollipop yarn, 18 sc (UK dc) in Natur yarn (50 sts).

Round 14: 18 sc (UK dc), dec 1 st in Natur yarn, 12 sc (UK dc) in Lollipop yarn, dec 1 st, 16 sc (UK dc) in Natur yarn (48 sts).

Round 15: 17 sc (UK dc), dec 1 st in Natur yarn, inc 1 st, 10 sc (UK dc), inc 1 st in Lollipop yarn, dec 1 st, 15 sc (UK dc) in Natur yarn (48 sts).

Round 16: 16 sc (UK dc), dec 1 st in Natur yarn, inc 1 st, 12 sc (UK dc), inc 1 st in Lollipop yarn, dec 1 st, 14 sc (UK dc) in Natur yarn (48 sts).

Fasten off the Natur yarn. Continue crocheting in Lollipop yarn:

Rounds 17–21: 1 sc (UK dc) into each st of previous round (48 sts).
Stuff the head.

Round 22: *6 sc (UK dc), dec 1 st*, rep from * to * five more times (42 sts).

Round 23: *5 sc (UK dc), dec 1 st*, rep from * to * five more times (36 sts).

Round 24: *4 sc (UK dc), dec 1 st*, rep from * to * five more times (30 sts).

Round 25: *3 sc (UK dc), dec 1 st*, rep from * to * five more times (24 sts).

Round 26: *2 sc (UK dc), dec 1 st*, rep from * to * five more times (18 sts).

Round 27: *1 sc (UK dc), dec 1 st*, rep from * to * five more times (12 sts).

Round 28: dec 1 st six times (6 sts).

Round 29: *skip 1 st, 1 sl st*, rep from * to * twice more (3 sts).
Secure the yarn and fasten off.

BODY
Work in rounds. At the end of each round, work 1 sl st into first st in round, 1 ch and but do not turn.

Round 1: using Lollipop yarn, work 6 sc (UK dc) into a magic ring (6 sts).

Round 2: inc 1 st six times (12 sts).

Round 3: 1 sc (UK dc) into each st of previous round (12 sts).

Round 4: *1 sc (UK dc), inc 1 st*, rep from * to * five more times (18 sts).

Change to Pink Lipstick yarn. Join Lollipop yarn in the round. Crochet around the yarn not currently being used. Take care not to pull the yarn too tight. At the end of each round, change to Pink Lipstick yarn.

Round 5: inc 1 st 15 times in Pink Lipstick yarn, inc 1 st three times in Lollipop yarn (36 sts).

Round 6: *5 sc (UK dc), inc 1 st*, rep from * to * four more times in Pink Lipstick yarn, 5 sc (UK dc), inc 1st in Lollipop yarn (42 sts).

Rounds 7–22: 35 sc (UK dc) in Pink Lipstick yarn, 7 sc (UK dc) in Lollipop yarn (42 sts).

Round 23: dec 1 st, 31 sc (UK dc), dec 1 st in Pink Lipstick yarn, inc 1 st, 5 sc (UK dc), inc 1 st in Lollipop yarn (42 sts).

Round 24: 33 sc (UK dc) in Pink Lipstick yarn, 9 sc (UK dc) in Lollipop yarn (42 sts).

Round 25: dec 1 st, 29 sc (UK dc), dec 1 st in Pink Lipstick yarn, inc 1 st, 7 sc (UK dc), inc 1 st in Lollipop yarn (42 sts).

Fasten off Pink Lipstick yarn and continue crocheting in Lollipop yarn:

Round 26: work into the back bar of the stitch only: 31 sc (UK dc) into both bars of the stitch: 11 sc (UK dc) (42 sts).

Rounds 27–33: 1 sc (UK dc) into each st of previous round (42 sts).

Stuff the body.

Round 34: *5 sc (UK dc), dec 1 st*, rep from * to * five more times (36 sts).

Round 35: *4 sc (UK dc), dec 1 st*, rep from * to * five more times (30 sts).

Round 36: *3 sc (UK dc), dec 1 st*, rep from * to * five more times (24 sts).

Round 37: *2 sc (UK dc), dec 1 st*, rep from * to * five more times (18 sts).

Round 38: *1 sc (UK dc), dec 1 st*, rep from * to * five more times (12 sts).

Round 39: dec 1 st six times (6 sts).

Round 40: *skip 1 st, 1 sl st*, rep from * to * twice more (3 sts).

Secure the yarn and fasten off.

LEGS (MAKE 2)

Work in spiral rounds. This means the rounds are not finished with a sl st, nor do you work a turning ch at the beg of a new round.

Round 1: using Brombeer yarn, work 6 sc (UK dc) into a magic ring (6 sts).

Round 2: inc 1 st six times (12 sts).

Rounds 3–5: 1 sc (UK dc) into each st of previous round (12 sts).

Change to Lollipop yarn.

Rounds 6–36: 1 sc (UK dc) into each st of previous round (12 sts).

Secure the yarn and fasten off. Stuff the leg.

ARMS (MAKE 2)

Work in spiral rounds. This means the rounds are not finished with a sl st, nor do you work a turning ch at the beg of a new round.

Round 1: using Brombeer yarn, work 6 sc (UK dc) into a magic ring (6 sts).

Round 2: inc 1 st six times (12 sts).

Rounds 3–5: 1 sc (UK dc) into each st of previous round (12 sts).

Secure Brombeer yarn and fasten off. Change to Natur yarn, and join in Lollipop yarn while you are working the round.

Rounds 6–12: 5 sc (UK dc) in Natur yarn, 7 sc (UK dc) in Lollipop yarn (12 sts).

Change to Pink Lipstick yarn.

Rounds 13–27: 1 sc (UK dc) into each st of previous round (12 sts).

Secure the yarn and fasten off. Stuff the arm three-quarters full.

EARS (MAKE 2)

Work in rounds. At the end of each round, work 1 sl st into first st in round, 1 ch and do not turn.

Round 1: using Brombeer yarn, work 6 sc (UK dc) into a magic ring (6 sts).

Round 2: 1 sc (UK dc) into each st of previous round (6 sts).

Round 3: inc 1 st six times (12 sts).

Round 4: 1 sc (UK dc) into each st of previous round (12 sts). Secure Brombeer yarn and fasten off.

Change to Lollipop yarn, then join in Natur yarn, changing back to Lollipop yarn while you are working the round.

Round 5: *1 sc (UK dc), inc 1 st*, rep from * to * twice more, 1 sc (UK dc) in Lollipop yarn, inc 1 st, 1 sc (UK dc), inc 1 st in Natur yarn, 1 sc (UK dc), inc 1 st in Lollipop yarn (18 sts).

Rounds 6–10: 10 sc (UK dc) in Lollipop yarn, 5 sc (UK dc) in Natur yarn, 3 sc (UK dc) in Lollipop yarn (18 sts).

Round 11: 10 sc (UK dc) in Lollipop yarn, dec 1 st, 1 sc (UK dc), dec 1 st in Natur yarn, 3 sc (UK dc) in Lollipop yarn (16 sts). Secure the yarn and fasten off. Do not stuff the ear.

EYES (MAKE 2)

Round 1: using Black yarn, work 6 sc (UK dc) into a magic ring (6 sts).
Join in the round with 1 sl st into the first st. Secure the yarn and fasten off.

FINISHING OFF

Press the last round of the ear together to bend it slightly. The part in Natur yarn should be on the inside. Using whip stitch, sew the edge to rounds 22 and 23 of the head. Sew the eyes under the arches on the sides of the head, and add two French knots to each eye with White yarn. Using Black yarn, sew two eyelashes beside the eyes. For the nose, sew horizontal lines to the head above the magic ring using Black yarn. Sew the magic ring of the body to the underside of the head using mattress stitch. For each arm, press the last round together, and sew to the side of the body at round 5. Make sure that the part of the arm in Natur yarn is facing the side of the body. To attach the legs, press the last round together and sew to the underside of the body.

Harry
THE RACCOON

Also known as the Einstein of the forest, Harry is the best mathematician in the area. He has taken part in numerous mental arithmetic championships all over the world and has won them all.

HEIGHT
★ Approx. 19½in (50cm)

MATERIAL
★ Lang Yarns Merino 120 (100% merino wool); 2 balls of Grey Mélange 0324, 1 ball each of Black 0004 and Cream 002; 50g/131yd/120m
★ Schachenmayr Catania (100% cotton); scraps of Blue Iris 384 or Turquoise 146; 50g/68yd/63m
★ 2.5mm (B-1/UK 13) crochet hook
★ Toy stuffing
★ Tapestry needle

HEAD
Work in rounds. At the end of each round, work 1 sl st into first st in round, 1 ch and turn.

Tip: For this pattern, the colours frequently change within a round. Crochet around the yarn not currently being used. However, only do this if you do not need this colour again in this row. If not, just leave it hanging so you can pick it up again on the return round. This will save you having to join new yarns.

Round 1: using Cream yarn, work 6 sc (UK dc) into a magic ring (6 sts).

Round 2: 1 sc (UK dc) into each st of previous round (6 sts).

Round 3: inc 1 st six times (12 sts).

Round 4: 1 sc (UK dc) into each st of previous round (12 sts).

Round 5: *1 sc (UK dc), inc 1 st*, rep from * to * 5 more times (18 sts).

Round 6: 1 sc (UK dc) into each st of previous round (18 sts).

Round 7: *2 sc (UK dc), inc 1 st*, rep from * to * five more times (24 sts).

Round 8: 1 sc (UK dc) into each st of previous round (24 sts).

Round 9: 3 sc (UK dc), inc 1 st, 3 sc (UK dc), inc 1 st, 2 sc (UK dc), change to Grey Mélange yarn, 1 sc (UK dc), inc 1 st twice, 1 sc (UK dc), change to Cream yarn, 2 sc (UK dc), inc 1 st, 3 sc (UK dc), inc 1 st, 3 sc (UK dc) (30 sts).

Round 10: 13 sc (UK dc) in Cream yarn, 6 sc (UK dc) in Grey Mélange yarn, 11 sc (UK dc) in Cream yarn (30 sts).

Round 11: 9 sc (UK dc), inc 1 st, 2 sc (UK dc) in Cream yarn, 6 sc (UK dc) in Grey Mélange yarn, 2 sc (UK dc), inc 1 st, 9 sc (UK dc) in Cream yarn (32 sts).

Round 12: 14 sc (UK dc) in Cream yarn, 6 sc (UK dc) in Grey Mélange yarn, 11 sc (UK dc) in Cream yarn (32 sts).

Round 13: 7 sc (UK dc), inc 1 st, 2 sc (UK dc), inc 1 st, 2 sc (UK dc) in Cream yarn, 6 sc (UK dc) in Grey Mélange yarn, 2 sc (UK dc), inc 1 st, 2 sc (UK dc), inc 1 st, 7 sc (UK dc) in Cream yarn (36 sts). Secure the Cream yarn and fasten off. Join in Black yarn to the first st and continue crocheting as follows:

Round 14: 16 sc (UK dc) in Black yarn, 6 sc (UK dc) in Grey Mélange yarn, 14 sc (UK dc) in Black yarn (36 sts).

Round 15: 3 sc (UK dc), inc 1 st, *1 sc (UK dc), inc 1 st*, rep from * to * four more times, 1 sc (UK dc) in Black yarn, 6 sc (UK dc) in Grey Mélange yarn, *1 sc (UK dc), inc 1 st*, rep from * to * five more times, 3 sc (UK dc) in Black yarn (48 sts).

Round 16: 22 sc (UK dc) in Black yarn, 6 sc (UK dc) in Grey Mélange yarn, 20 sc (UK dc) in Black yarn (48 sts).

Round 17: *8 sc (UK dc), inc 1 st*, rep from * to * once more, 3 sc (UK dc) in Black yarn, 6 sc (UK dc) in Grey Mélange yarn, 3 sc (UK dc), *inc 1 st, 8 sc (UK dc)*, rep from * to * once more in Black yarn (52 sts).

Round 18: 24 sc (UK dc) in Black yarn, inc 1 st six times in Grey Mélange yarn, 22 sc (UK dc) in Black yarn (58 sts).

Round 19: 23 sc (UK dc) in Black yarn, 1 sc (UK dc), inc 1 st, 8 sc (UK dc), inc 1 st, 1 sc (UK dc) in Grey Mélange yarn, 23 sc (UK dc) in Black yarn (60 sts).

Round 20: 24 sc (UK dc) in Black yarn, 1 sc (UK dc), inc 1 st, 10 sc (UK dc), inc 1 st, 1 sc (UK dc) in Grey Mélange yarn, 22 sc (UK dc) in Black yarn (62 sts).

Round 21: 23 sc (UK dc) in Black yarn, 16 sc (UK dc) in Grey Mélange yarn, 23 sc (UK dc) in Black yarn (62 sts). Secure Black yarn and fasten off. Join Grey Mélange yarn to the first st and continue crocheting as follows.

Round 22: 12 sc (UK dc) in Grey Mélange yarn, 12 sc (UK dc) in Cream yarn, 16 sc (UK dc) in Grey Mélange yarn, 12 sc (UK dc) in Cream yarn, 10 sc (UK dc) in Grey Mélange yarn (62 sts).

Round 23: 11 sc (UK dc) in Grey Mélange yarn, 12 sc (UK dc) in Cream yarn, 16 sc (UK dc) in Grey Mélange yarn, 12 sc (UK dc) in Cream yarn, 11 sc (UK dc) in Grey Mélange yarn (62 sts).

Round 24: 12 sc (UK dc) in Grey Mélange yarn, 12 sc (UK dc) in Cream yarn, 16 sc (UK dc) in Grey Mélange yarn, 12 sc (UK dc) in Cream yarn, 10 sc (UK dc) in Grey Mélange yarn (62 sts).

Round 25: 11 sc (UK dc) in Grey Mélange yarn, 12 sc (UK dc) in Cream yarn, 16 sc (UK dc) in Grey Mélange yarn, 12 sc (UK dc) in Cream yarn, 11 sc (UK dc) in Grey Mélange yarn (62 sts). Secure the Cream yarn and fasten off. Continue working in Grey Mélange yarn.

Round 26: 1 sc (UK dc) into each st of previous round (62 sts).

Round 27: 11 sc (UK dc), inc 1 st, 10 sc (UK dc), inc 1 st, 16 sc (UK dc), inc 1 st, 10 sc (UK dc), inc 1 st, 11 sc (UK dc) (66 sts).

Round 28: 13 sc (UK dc), inc 1 st, 10 sc (UK dc), inc 1 st, 4 sc (UK dc), inc 1 st, 8 sc (UK dc), inc 1 st, 4 sc (UK dc), inc 1 st, 10 sc (UK dc), inc 1 st, 11 sc (UK dc) (72 sts).

Round 29: *11 sc (UK dc), inc 1 st*, rep from * to * five more times (78 sts).

Rounds 30–33: 1 sc (UK dc) into each st of previous round (78 sts).

Round 34: *11 sc (UK dc), dec 1 st*, rep from * to * five more times (72 sts).

Round 35: *10 sc (UK dc), dec 1 st*, rep from * to * five more times (66 sts).

Round 36: *9 sc (UK dc), dec 1 st*, rep from * to * five more times (60 sts).

Round 37: *8 sc (UK dc), dec 1 st*, rep from * to * five more times (54 sts).

Stuff the head.

Round 38: *7 sc (UK dc), dec 1 st*, rep from * to * five more times (48 sts).

Round 39: *6 sc (UK dc), dec 1 st*, rep from * to * five more times (42 sts).

Round 40: *5 sc (UK dc), dec 1 st*, rep from * to * five more times (36 sts).

Round 41: *4 sc (UK dc), dec 1 st*, rep from * to * five more times (30 sts).

Round 42: *3 sc (UK dc), dec 1 st*, rep from * to * five more times (24 sts).

Round 43: *2 sc (UK dc), dec 1 st*, rep from * to * five more times (18 sts).

Round 44: *1 sc (UK dc), dec 1 st*, rep from * to * five more times (12 sts).

Round 45: dec 1 st six times (6 sts).

Round 46: *skip 1 st, 1 sl st*, rep from * to * twice more (3 sts).

Secure the yarn and fasten off.

BODY

Work in rounds. At the end of each round, work 1 sl st into first st in round, 1 ch and turn.

Round 1: using Grey Mélange yarn, work 6 sc (UK dc) into a magic ring (6 sts).

Round 2: inc 1 st six times (12 sts).

Round 3: *1 sc (UK dc), inc 1 st*, rep from * to * five more times (18 sts).

Round 4: *2 sc (UK dc), inc 1 st*, rep from * to * five more times (24 sts).

Round 5: *3 sc (UK dc), inc 1 st*, rep from * to * five more times (30 sts).

Round 6: *4 sc (UK dc), inc 1 st*, rep from * to * five more times (36 sts).

Round 7: *5 sc (UK dc), inc 1 st*, rep from * to * five more times (42 sts).

Round 8: *6 sc (UK dc), inc 1 st*, rep from * to * five more times (48 sts).

Round 9: *7 sc (UK dc), inc 1 st*, rep from * to * five more times (54 sts).

Round 10: *8 sc (UK dc), inc 1 st*, rep from * to * five more times (60 sts).

Round 11: *9 sc (UK dc), inc 1 st*, rep from * to * five more times (66 sts).

Rounds 12–22: 1 sc (UK dc) into each st of previous round (66 sts).

Round 23: *9 sc (UK dc), dec 1 st*, rep from * to * five more times (60 sts).

Rounds 24–31: 1 sc (UK dc) into each st of previous round (60 sts).

Round 32: *8 sc (UK dc), dec 1 st*, rep from * to * five more times (54 sts).

Rounds 33–46: 1 sc (UK dc) into each st of previous round (54 sts).

Round 47: *7 sc (UK dc), dec 1 st*, rep from * to * five more times (48 sts).

Round 48: *6 sc (UK dc), dec 1 st*, rep from * to * five more times (42 sts).

Round 49: *5 sc (UK dc), dec 1 st*, rep from * to * five more times (36 sts).

Secure the yarn and fasten off. Stuff the body.

ARMS (MAKE 2)

Work in rounds. At the end of each round, work 1 sl st into first st in round, 1 ch and turn.

Round 1: using Black yarn, work 6 sc (UK dc) into a magic ring (6 sts).

Rounds 2–10: 1 sc (UK dc) into each st of previous round (6 sts).

Change to Grey Mélange yarn.

Rounds 11–31: 1 sc (UK dc) into each st of previous round (6 sts).

Secure the yarn and fasten off. Do not stuff the arm.

LEGS (MAKE 2)

Work in rounds. At the end of each round, work 1 sl st into first st in round, 1 ch and turn.

Round 1: using Black yarn, work 6 sc (UK dc) into a magic ring (6 sts).

Round 2: *1 sc (UK dc), inc 1 st*, rep from * to * twice more (9 sts).

Rounds 3–14: 1 sc (UK dc) into each st of previous round (9 sts).

Change to Grey Mélange yarn.

Rounds 15–47: 1 sc (UK dc) into each st of previous round (9 sts).

Secure the yarn and fasten off. Loosely stuff.

TAIL

Work in rounds. At the end of each round, work 1 sl st into first st in round, 1 ch and turn.

Round 1: using Black yarn, work 6 sc (UK dc) into a magic ring (6 sts).

Round 2: inc 1 st six times (12 sts).

Rounds 3 and 4: 1 sc (UK dc) into each st of previous round (12 sts).

Round 5: *1 sc (UK dc), inc 1 st*, rep from * to * five more times (18 sts).

Round 6: 1 sc (UK dc) into each st of previous round (18 sts).

Change to Grey Mélange yarn.

Rounds 7 and 8: 1 sc (UK dc) into each st of previous round (18 sts).

Round 9: *2 sc (UK dc), inc 1 st*, rep from * to * five more times (24 sts).

Round 10: 1 sc (UK dc) into each st of previous round (24 sts).

Round 11: *3 sc (UK dc), inc 1 st*, rep from * to * five more times (30 sts).

Round 12: 1 sc (UK dc) into each st of previous round (30 sts).

Change to Black yarn.

Round 13: *4 sc (UK dc), inc 1 st*, rep from * to * five more times (36 sts).

Rounds 14–18: 1 sc (UK dc) into each st of previous round (36 sts).

Change to Grey Mélange yarn.

Rounds 19–24: 1 sc (UK dc) into each st of previous round (36 sts).

Change to Black yarn.

Round 25: *10 sc (UK dc), dec 1 st*, rep from * to * twice more (33 sts).

Rounds 26–28: 1 sc (UK dc) into each st of previous round (33 sts).

Round 29: *9 sc (UK dc), dec 1 st*, rep from * to * twice more (30 sts).

Round 30: 1 sc (UK dc) into each st of previous round (30 sts).

Stuff the tail. Change to Grey Mélange yarn.

Rounds 31 and 32: 1 sc (UK dc) into each st of previous round (30 sts).
Round 33: *3 sc (UK dc), dec 1 st*, rep from * to * five more times (24 sts).
Rounds 34–36: 1 sc (UK dc) in each st of previous round (24 sts).
Change to Black yarn.
Round 37: *2 sc (UK dc), dec 1 st*, rep from * to * five more times (18 sts).
Rounds 38–42: 1 sc (UK dc) into each st of previous round (18 sts).
Change to Grey Mélange yarn.
Round 43: *1 sc (UK dc), dec 1 st*, rep from * to * five more times (12 sts).
Rounds 44–48: 1 sc (UK dc) into each st of previous round (12 sts).
Secure the yarn and fasten off. Stuff the remainder of the tail.

EARS (MAKE 2 GREY MÉLANGE, 2 CREAM)

Work in rows. At the end of each row, work 1 ch to turn.
Row 1: work 17 ch, 1 sc (UK dc) into second ch from hook, 5 sc (UK dc), dec 1 st twice, 6 sc (UK dc) (14 sts).
Rows 2 and 3: 1 sc (UK dc) into each st of previous row (14 sts).

Row 4: 5 sc (UK dc), dec 1 st twice, 5 sc (UK dc) (12 sts).
Rows 5–7: 1 sc (UK dc) into each st of previous row (12 sts).
Row 8: 4 sc (UK dc), dec 1 st twice, 4 sc (UK dc) (10 sts).
Rows 9–11: 1 sc (UK dc) into each st of previous row (10 sts).
Row 12: 3 sc (UK dc), dec 1 st twice, 3 sc (UK dc) (8 sts).
Row 13: 1 sc (UK dc) into each st of previous row (8 sts).
Row 14: 2 sc (UK dc), dec 1 st twice, 2 sc (UK dc) (6 sts).
Row 15: dec 1 st twice (4 sts).
Row 16: dec 1 st twice (2 sts).
Secure the yarn and fasten off. Place one grey mélange and one cream ear together, join Black yarn to bottom right corner and sc (UK dc) them together – do not crochet around the side that is used to sew the ear to the head. Work 1 ch at bottom left corner, turn and work another row of sc (UK dc).

NOSE

Work in rows. At the end of each row, work 1 ch to turn.
Row 1: using Black yarn, work 5 ch, 1 sc (UK dc) into second ch from the hook, 1 sc (UK dc) into remaining ch (4 sts).
Row 2: 1 sc (UK dc) into each st of previous row (4 sts).
Row 3: 1 sc (UK dc), dec 1 st, 1 sc (UK dc) (3 sts).
Row 4: 1 sc (UK dc) into each st of previous row (3 sts)
Row 5: work 3 sc (UK dc) tog (1 st).
Do not fasten off, but work two rounds sc (UK dc) around the emerging triangle
Secure the yarn and fasten off.

EYES (MAKE 2)

Round 1: using Black yarn, work 6 sc (UK dc) into a magic ring (6 sts).
Join in a round with 1 sl st into the first st. Change to Blue Iris yarn.
Round 2: *1 sc (UK dc), inc 1 st*, rep from * to * twice more (9 sts).
Join in a round with 1 sl st into the first st of the round.
Secure the yarn and fasten off.

FINISHING OFF

Sew the last round of the body to the underside of the head using whip stitch. Attach the nose above the magic ring of the head. Sew the eyes to the sides of the head at rounds 16–18, and embroider two French knots in Cream yarn to each pupil. Join Black yarn to a cream area at the top of the face, and work along the edge in sc (UK dc). Sew the ears to the side of the back of the head using whip stitch. Sew the last round of each arm to the sides of the body at round 36 using whip stitch. Sew the last round of each leg to the side of the body at rounds 8–10 using whip stitch. Sew the last round of the tail to the back of the body at rounds 21 and 22.

Winnie
THE RABBIT

As a baby bunny, Winnie ate too much beetroot – and it turned her cheeks pink! They are still that way now she's grown. Carrots are her favourites now, but occasionally she still treats herself to a few beetroot slices.

HEIGHT
★ Approx. 15¾in (40cm)

MATERIALS
★ Austermann Merino 160 (100% merino wool); 2 balls of Hemp 215, 1 ball of Rosa 211, and scraps of Dark Brown 206 and White 201; 50g/174yd/160m
★ 2.5mm (B-1/UK 13) crochet hook
★ Toy stuffing
★ Tapestry needle

BODY
Work in spiral rounds. This means the rounds are not finished with a sl st, nor do you work a turning ch at the beg of a new round.

Round 1: using Hemp yarn, work 6 sc (UK dc) into a magic ring (6 sts).

Round 2: inc 1 st six times (12 sts).

Round 3: *1 sc (UK dc), inc 1 st*, rep from * to * five more times (18 sts).

Round 4: *2 sc (UK dc), inc 1 st*, rep from * to * five more times (24 sts).

Round 5: *3 sc (UK dc), inc 1 st*, rep from * to * five more times (30 sts).

Round 6: *4 sc (UK dc), inc 1 st*, rep from * to * five more times (36 sts).

Round 7: *5 sc (UK dc), inc 1 st*, rep from * to * five more times (42 sts).

Round 8: *6 sc (UK dc), inc 1 st*, rep from * to * five more times (48 sts).

Round 9: *7 sc (UK dc), inc 1 st*, rep from * to * five more times (54 sts).

Rounds 10–21: 1 sc (UK dc) into each st of previous round (54 sts).

Round 22: *7 sc (UK dc), dec 1 st*, rep from * to * five more times (48 sts).

Rounds 23–28: 1 sc (UK dc) into each st of previous round (48 sts).

Round 29: *6 sc (UK dc), dec 1 st*, rep from * to * five more times (42 sts).

Rounds 30–35: 1 sc (UK dc) into each st of previous round (42 sts).

Round 36: *5 sc (UK dc), dec 1 st*, rep from * to * five more times (36 sts).

Rounds 37–40: 1 sc (UK dc) into each st of previous round (36 sts). Stuff the body.

Round 41: *4 sc (UK dc), dec 1 st*, rep from * to * five more times (30 sts).

Round 42: *3 sc (UK dc), dec 1 st*, rep from * to * five more times (24 sts).

Round 43: *2 sc (UK dc), dec 1 st*, rep from * to * five more times (18 sts). Secure the yarn and fasten off.

HEAD
Work in spiral rounds. This means the rounds are not finished with a sl st, nor do you work a turning ch at the beg of a new round.

Round 1: using Hemp yarn, work 6 sc (UK dc) into a magic ring (6 sts).

Round 2: inc 1 st six times (12 sts).

Round 3: *1 sc (UK dc), inc 1 st*, rep from * to * five more times (18 sts).

Round 4: *2 sc (UK dc), inc 1 st*, rep from * to * five more times (24 sts).

Round 5: *3 sc (UK dc), inc 1 st*, rep from * to * five more times (30 sts).

Rounds 6–9: 1 sc (UK dc) into each st of previous round (30 sts).

Round 10: *4 sc (UK dc), inc 1 st*, rep from * to * five more times (36 sts).

Rounds 11–13: 1 sc (UK dc) into each st of previous round (36 sts).

Round 14: *5 sc (UK dc), inc 1 st*, rep from * to * five more times (42 sts).

Rounds 15–19: 1 sc (UK dc) into each st of previous round (42 sts).

Round 20: *inc 1 st, 3 sc (UK dc)*, rep from * to * twice more, 30 sc (UK dc) (45 sts).

Round 21: *inc 1 st, 4 sc (UK dc)*, rep from * to * twice more, 30 sc (UK dc) (48 sts).

The inc of the last two rounds will be at the top of the finished rabbit's nose.

Rounds 22–26: 1 sc (UK dc) into each st of previous round (48 sts).

Round 27: *6 sc (UK dc), dec 1 st*, rep from * to * five more times (42 sts). Stuff the head.

Round 28: *5 sc (UK dc), dec 1 st*, rep from * to * five more times (36 sts).

Round 29: *4 sc (UK dc), dec 1 st*, rep from * to * five more times (30 sts).

Round 30: *3 sc (UK dc), dec 1 st*, rep from * to * five more times (24 sts).

Round 31: *2 sc (UK dc), dec 1 st*, rep from * to * five more times (18 sts).

Round 32: *1 sc (UK dc), dec 1 st*, rep from * to * five more times (12 sts).

Round 33: dec 1 st six times (6 sts).

Round 34: *skip 1 st, 1 sl st*, rep from * to * twice more (3 sts).

Secure the yarn and fasten off.

EARS (MAKE 2)

Work in rows. At the end of each row, work 1 ch and turn.

Row 1: using Rosa yarn, work 17 ch, 1 sc (UK dc) into second ch from hook, 3 sc (UK dc), 4 hdc (UK htr), 7 dc (UK tr), 6 dc (UK tr) into last st. Continue working on the other side of the length of ch: 7 dc (UK tr), 4 hdc (UK htr), 4 sc (UK dc) (36 sts).

Row 2: 4 sc (UK dc), 4 hdc (UK htr), 7 dc (UK tr), 2 dc (UK tr) in 1 st six times, 7 dc (UK tr), 4 hdc (UK htr), 4 sc (UK dc) (42 sts).

Secure the yarn and fasten off. Repeat rows 1 and 2 with Hemp yarn. Do not fasten off the yarn this time. Place the two parts of the ear together and hold the work with Rosa yarn piece showing.

Row 3: using Hemp yarn crochet the ear pieces together with 1 sc (UK dc) into each st of previous row (42 sts).

Rows 4 and 5: 1 sc (UK dc) into each st of previous row (42 sts).

Secure the yarn and fasten off.

ARMS (MAKE 2)
PAW

Work in rounds. At the end of each round, work 1 sl st into first st in round, 1 ch and turn. Work following st into a magic ring in Rosa yarn:

Round 1: 1 sc (UK dc), 1 hdc (UK htr), 1 dc (UK tr), 1 hdc (UK htr), 2 sc (UK dc), 1 hdc (UK htr), 1 dc (UK tr), 1 hdc (UK htr), 1 sc (UK dc) (10 sts).

Round 2: 1 sc (UK dc), inc 1 st three times, 2 sc (UK dc), inc 1 st three times, 1 sc (UK dc) (16 sts).

Change to Hemp yarn.

Round 3: work into the back bar of the stitch only: *3 sc (UK dc), inc 1 st*, rep from * to * three more times (20 sts).

Round 4: 2 sc (UK dc), skip 4 st, 14 sc (UK dc) (20 sts).

Stuff the paw.

Round 5: 13 sc (UK dc), dec 1 st twice, 3 sc (UK dc) (18 sts).

Round 6: *1 sc (UK dc), dec 1 st*, rep from * to * five more times (12 sts).

Round 7: dec 1 st six times (6 sts).

Round 8: *skip 1 st, 1 sl st*, rep from * to * twice more (3 sts).

Secure the yarn and fasten off.

Round 1: Join Hemp yarn to first skipped st in round 4 of paw and work 12 sc (UK dc) in gap. Work in spiral rounds. This means the rounds are not finished with a sl st, nor do you work a turning ch at the beg of a new round (12 sts).

Round 2: *2 sc (UK dc), dec 1 st*, rep from * to * twice more (9 sts).

Rounds 3–23: 1 sc (UK dc) into each st of previous round (9 sts).

Secure the yarn and fasten off. Stuff the arm.

LEGS (MAKE 2)

Round 1: work 11 ch in Hemp yarn, 1 sc (UK dc) into second ch from hook, 1 sc (UK dc) into next 8 ch, 4 sc (UK dc) into last ch. Continue working on the other side of the length of ch: 8 sc (UK dc), 3 sc (UK dc) into ch with first st (24 sts).

Round 2: inc 1 st, 2 sc (UK dc), 2 hdc (UK htr), 3 dc (UK tr), 2 dc (UK tr) in 1 st twice, 3 dc (UK tr), 2 hdc (UK htr), 2 sc (UK dc), inc 1 st, 2 sc (UK dc) (32 sts).

Round 3: inc 1 st twice, 2 sc (UK dc), 2 hdc (UK htr), 5 dc (UK tr), 2 dc (UK tr) in 1 st eight times, 5 dc (UK tr), 2 hdc (UK htr), 2 sc (UK dc), inc 1 st twice, 2 sc (UK dc) (44 sts).

Round 4: work into the back bar of the stitch only: 1 sc (UK dc) into each st of previous round (44 sts).

Round 5: 1 sc (UK dc) into each st of previous round (44 sts).

Round 6: 11 sc (UK dc), 22 dc (UK tr), 11 sc (UK dc) (44 sts).

Round 7: 11 sc (UK dc), *skip 1 st, 1 sc (UK dc)*, rep from * to * ten more times, 11 sc (UK dc) (33 sts).

Round 8 (left leg): 11 sc (UK dc), 5 dc (UK tr), 2 dc (UK tr) tog, 4 dc (UK tr), 11 sc (UK dc) (32 sts).

Round 9 (right leg): 11 sc (UK dc), 4 dc (UK tr), 2 dc (UK tr) tog, 5 dc (UK tr), 11 sc (UK dc) (32 sts).

Round 10: 11 sc (UK dc), *skip 1 st, 1 sc (UK dc)*, rep from * to * four more times, 11 sc (UK dc) (27 sts).

Round 11: 11 sc (UK dc), dec 1 st, 1 sc (UK dc), dec 1 st, 11 sc (UK dc) (25 sts).

Round 12: 1 sc (UK dc), dec 1 st, 23 sc (UK dc) (24 sts).

Round 13: *2 sc (UK dc), dec 1 st*, rep from * to * five more times (18 sts).

Rounds 14–39: 1 sc (UK dc) into each st of previous round (18 sts).

Secure the yarn and fasten off. Stuff the leg.

EYES (MAKE 2)

Round 1: using Dark Brown yarn, work 6 sc (UK dc) into a magic ring (6 sts).

Join in a round with 1 sl st into the first st. Secure the yarn and fasten off.

PINK CHEEKS

Work following st into a magic ring using Rosa yarn: 1 sc (UK dc), 1 hdc (UK htr), 1 dc (UK tr), 1 hdc (UK htr), 2 sc (UK dc), 1 hdc (UK htr), 1 dc (UK tr), 1 hdc (UK htr), 1 sc (UK dc). Join in a round with 1 sl st into the first st.
Secure the yarn and fasten off.

FINISHING OFF

Hold the head so that the inc of rounds 20 and 21 are facing up and sew the narrow end of each ear to rounds 29–31 using whip stitch. Sew the pink cheeks on the sides of the head to rounds 20–23. Sew the eyes to the top of the head, above the pink cheeks. Using White yarn, embroider two French knots to each eye. Sew two eyelashes in Dark Brown yarn beside each eye. For the nose, sew a few horizontal stitches at round 3 of the head with Dark Brown yarn. Sew the last row of the body to the underside of the head using whip stitch. For each arm, press the last round together and use whip stitch to sew to the side of the body at round 42. Sew the last round of each leg to the underside of the body using whip stitch, making sure the foot is pointing up.

FARM

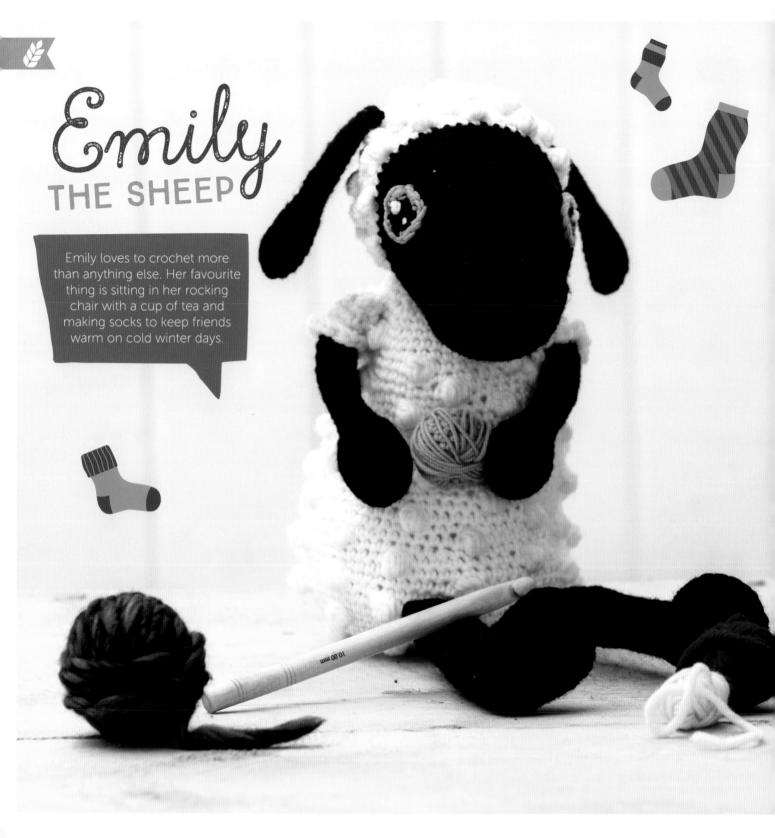

Emily
THE SHEEP

Emily loves to crochet more than anything else. Her favourite thing is sitting in her rocking chair with a cup of tea and making socks to keep friends warm on cold winter days.

Let's Go

HEIGHT
★ Approx. 13in (33cm)

MATERIALS
★ Lana Grossa Cool Wool Big (100% merino wool); 2 balls of White 601, 1 ball of Black 627, and scraps of Green 941; 50g/131yd/120m
★ Lang Yarns Merino 120 (100% merino wool); scraps of Pink 0085; 50g/131yd/120m
★ 2.5mm (B-1/UK 13) crochet hook
★ Toy stuffing
★ Tapestry needle

HEAD
Work in rounds. At the end of each round, work 1 sl st into first st in round, 1 ch and turn.

Round 1: work 8 ch in Black yarn, 1 sc (UK dc) into second ch from hook, 1 sc (UK dc) into each of next 5 ch, 4 sc (UK dc) into last ch. Continue working on the other side of the length of ch: 5 sc (UK dc), 3 sc (UK dc) into ch with first st (18 sts).

Round 2: inc 1 st, 5 sc (UK dc), inc 1 st four times, 5 sc (UK dc), inc 1 st three times (26 sts).

Round 3: 1 sc (UK dc) into each st of previous round (26 sts).

Round 4: inc 1 st, 8 sc (UK dc), inc 1 st, 3 sc (UK dc), inc 1 st, 8 sc (UK dc), inc 1 st, 3 sc (UK dc) (30 sts).

Rounds 5–11: 1 sc (UK dc) into each st of previous round (30 sts).

Round 12: inc 1 st, *2 sc (UK dc), inc 1 st*, rep from * to * four more times, 14 sc (UK dc) (36 sts).

Round 13: inc 1 st, *3 sc (UK dc), inc 1 st*, rep from * to * four more times, 15 sc (UK dc) (42 sts).

Round 14: inc 1 st, *4 sc (UK dc), inc 1 st*, rep from * to * four more times, 16 sc (UK dc) (48 sts).

Rounds 15–21: 1 sc (UK dc) in each st of previous round (48 sts).
Change to White yarn.

Round 22: 1 sc (UK dc) into each st of previous round (48 sts).

Round 23: 2 sc (UK dc), MB, *3 sc (UK dc), MB*, rep from * to * ten more times, 1 sc (UK dc) (48 sts).

Round 24: 1 sc (UK dc) into each st of previous round (48 sts).

Round 25: *MB, 3 sc (UK dc)*, rep from * to * eleven more times (48 sts).

Round 26: 1 sc (UK dc) into each st of previous round (48 sts).

Round 27: *3 sc (UK dc), MB*, rep from * to * eleven more times (48 sts).

Round 28: *6 sc (UK dc), dec 1 st*, rep from * to * five more times (42 sts).

Round 29: 1 sc (UK dc), MB, 3 sc (UK dc), MB, 2 sc (UK dc), MB, 4 sc (UK dc), MB, 2 sc (UK dc), MB, 2 sc (UK dc), MB, 3 sc (UK dc), MB, 2 sc (UK dc), MB, 3 sc (UK dc), MB, 2 sc (UK dc), MB, 1 sc (UK dc) (42 sts).

Round 30: *5 sc (UK dc), dec 1 st*, rep from * to * twice more (36 sts).

Round 31: MB, 2 sc (UK dc), MB, 2 sc (UK dc), MB, 3 sc (UK dc), MB, *2 sc (UK dc), MB*, rep from * to * seven more times, 1 sc (UK dc) (36 sts).
Stuff the head.

Round 32: *4 sc (UK dc), dec 1 st*, rep from * to * five more times (30 sts).

Round 33: *2 sc (UK dc), MB*, rep from * to * nine more times (30 sts).

Round 34: *3 sc (UK dc), dec 1 st*, rep from * to * five more times (24 sts).

Round 35: 1 sc (UK dc), MB, 2 sc (UK dc), MB, 3 sc (UK dc), MB, 2 sc (UK dc), MB, 3 sc (UK dc), MB, 2 sc (UK dc), MB, 4 sc (UK dc), MB (24 sts).

Round 36: *2 sc (UK dc), dec 1 st*, rep from * to * five more times (18 sts).

Round 37: *1 sc (UK dc), dec 1 st*, rep from * to * five more times (12 sts).

Round 38: dec 1 st six times (6 sts).

Round 39: *skip 1 st, 1 sl st*, rep from * to * twice more (3 sts).
Secure the yarn and fasten off.

BODY
Work in rounds. At the end of each round, work 1 sl st into first st in round, 1 ch and turn.

Round 1: using White yarn, work 6 sc (UK dc) into a magic ring (6 sts).

Round 2: inc 1 st six times (12 st).

Round 3: *1 sc (UK dc), inc 1 st*, rep from * to * five more times (18 sts).

Round 4: *2 sc (UK dc), inc 1 st*, rep from * to * five more times (24 sts).

Round 5: *3 sc (UK dc), inc 1 st*, rep from * to * five more times (30 sts).

Round 6: *2 sc (UK dc), MB, 1 sc (UK dc), inc 1 st*, rep from * to * five more times (36 sts).

Round 7: *5 sc (UK dc), inc 1 st*, rep from * to * five more times (42 sts).

Round 8: *6 sc (UK dc), inc 1 st*, rep from * to * five more times (48 sts).

Round 9: *MB, 6 sc (UK dc), inc 1 st*, rep from * to * five more times (54 sts).

Round 10: *8 sc (UK dc), inc 1 st*, rep from * to * five more times (60 sts).

Round 11: *9 sc (UK dc), inc 1 st*, rep from * to * five more times (66 sts).

Round 12: 5 sc (UK dc), MB, *10 sc (UK dc), MB*, rep from * to * four more times, 5 sc (UK dc) (66 sts).

Round 13: 1 sc (UK dc) into each st of previous round (66 sts).

Round 14: *MB, 10 sc (UK dc)*, rep from * to * five more times (66 sts).

Round 15: 1 sc (UK dc) into each st of previous round (66 sts).

Round 16: 5 sc (UK dc), MB, *10 sc (UK dc), MB*, rep from * to * four more times, 5 sc (UK dc) (66 sts).

Round 17: 1 sc (UK dc) into each st of previous round (66 sts).

Round 18: *MB, 10 sc (UK dc)*, rep from * to * five more times (66 sts).

Round 19: 7 sc (UK dc), dec 1 st, *9 sc (UK dc), dec 1 st*, rep from * to * four more times, 2 sc (UK dc) (60 sts).

Round 20: 5 sc (UK dc), MB, *9 sc (UK dc), MB*, rep from * to * four more times, 4 sc (UK dc) (60 sts).

Round 21: 1 sc (UK dc) into each st of previous round (60 sts).

Round 22: *MB, 9 sc (UK dc)*, rep from * to * five more times (60 sts).

Round 23: 4 sc (UK dc), dec 1 st, *8 sc (UK dc), dec 1 st*, rep from * to * four more times, 4 sc (UK dc) (54 sts).

Round 24: 4 sc (UK dc), MB, *8 sc (UK dc), MB*, rep from * to * four more times, 4 sc (UK dc) (54 sts).

Round 25: 1 sc (UK dc) into each st of previous round (54 sts).

Round 26: *MB, 8 sc (UK dc)*, rep from * to * five more times (54 sts).

Round 27: 5 sc (UK dc), dec 1 st, *7 sc (UK dc), dec 1 st*, rep from * to * four more times, 2 sc (UK dc) (48 sts).

Round 28: 4 sc (UK dc), MB, *7 sc (UK dc), MB*, rep from * to * four more times, 3 sc (UK dc) (48 sts).

Round 29: 1 sc (UK dc) into each st of previous round (48 sts).

Round 30: *MB, 7 sc (UK dc)*, rep from * to * five more times (48 sts).

Round 31: 2 sc (UK dc), dec 1 st, *6 sc (UK dc), dec 1 st*, rep from * to * four more times, 4 sc (UK dc) (42 sts).

Round 32: 3 sc (UK dc), MB, *6 sc (UK dc), MB*, rep from * to * three more times, 4 sc (UK dc) (42 sts).

Round 33: 1 sc (UK dc) into each st of previous round (42 sts).

Round 34: *MB, 6 sc (UK dc)*, rep from * to * five more times (42 sts).

Round 35: 1 sc (UK dc) into each st of previous round (42 sts).

Round 36: 3 sc (UK dc), MB, *6 sc (UK dc), MB*, rep from * to * three more times, 4 sc (UK dc) (42 sts).

Round 37: 1 sc (UK dc) into each st of previous round (42 sts).

Round 38: *MB, 6 sc (UK dc)*, rep from * to * five more times (42 sts).

Round 39: 1 sc (UK dc) into each st of previous round (42 sts).

Stuff the body.

Round 40: *5 sc (UK dc), dec 1 st*, rep from * to * five more times (36 sts).

Round 41: 1 sc (UK dc) into each st of previous round (36 sts).

Round 42: *4 sc (UK dc), dec 1 st*, rep from * to * five more times (30 sts).

Round 43: *3 sc (UK dc), dec 1 st*, rep from * to * five more times (24 sts).

Stuff the remainder of the body.

Round 44: 1 sc (UK dc) into each st of previous round (24 sts).

Round 45: *2 sc (UK dc), dec 1 st*, rep from * to * five more times (18 sts).

Round 46: *1 sc (UK dc), dec 1 st*, rep from * to * five more times (12 sts).

Round 47: dec 1 st six times (6 sts).

Round 48: *skip 1 st, 1 sl st*, rep from * to * twice more (3 sts).

Secure the yarn and fasten off.

ARMS (MAKE 2)

Work in spiral rounds. This means the rounds are not finished with a sl st, nor do you work a turning ch at the beg of a new round.

Round 1: using Black yarn, work 6 sc (UK dc) into a magic ring (6 sts).

Round 2: inc 1 st six times (12 st).

Round 3: *1 sc (UK dc), inc 1 st*, rep from * to * five more times (18 sts).

Rounds 4–7: 1 sc (UK dc) into each st of previous round (18 sts).

Round 8: *1 sc (UK dc), dec 1 st*, rep from * to * five more times (12 sts).

Round 9: *2 sc (UK dc), dec 1 st*, rep from * to * twice more (9 sts).

Rounds 10–22: 1 sc (UK dc) into each st of previous round (9 sts).

Change to White yarn.

Round 23: 1 sc (UK dc) into each st of previous round (9 sts).

Round 24: work into the back bar of the stitch only: inc 1 st nine times (18 sts).

Rounds 25–27: 1 sc (UK dc) into each st of previous round (18 sts).

Round 28: *1 sc (UK dc), dec 1 st*, rep from * to * five more times (12 sts).

Secure the yarn and fasten off. Stuff the arm.

LEGS (MAKE 2)

Work in rounds. At the end of each round, work 1 sl st into first st in round, 1 ch and turn.

Round 1: work 7 ch in Black yarn, 1 sc (UK dc) into second ch from hook, 1 sc (UK dc) into each of next 4 ch, 3 sc (UK dc) into last ch. Continue working on the other side of the length of ch: 4 sc (UK dc), 2 sc (UK dc) into first st (14 sts).

Round 2: inc 1 st, 4 sc (UK dc), inc 1 st three times, 4 sc (UK dc), inc 1 st twice (20 sts).

Round 3: inc 1 st, 4 sc (UK dc), 1 hdc (UK htr), 2 dc (UK tr) in 1 st six times, 1 hdc (UK htr), 4 sc (UK dc), inc 1 st, 2 sc (UK dc) (28 sts).

Round 4: 1 raised sc (UK dc) from the back of each st of previous round (28 sts).

Rounds 5 and 6: 1 sc (UK dc) into each st of previous round (28 sts).

Round 7: 3 sc (UK dc), dec 1 st ten times, 5 sc (UK dc) (18 sts).

Round 8: 1 sc (UK dc) into each st of previous round (18 sts).

Round 9: 4 sc (UK dc), dec 1 st four times, 6 sc (UK dc) (14 sts).

Rounds 10–35: 1 sc (UK dc) into each st of previous round (14 sts).

Secure the yarn and fasten off. Stuff the leg.

EARS (MAKE 2)

Work in spiral rounds. This means the rounds are not finished with a sl st, nor do you work a turning ch at the beg of a new round.

Round 1: using Black yarn, work 6 sc (UK dc) into a magic ring (6 sts).

Round 2: inc 1 st six times (12 st).

Round 3: *1 sc (UK dc), inc 1 st*, rep from * to * five more times (18 sts).

Rounds 4–7: 1 sc (UK dc) into each st of previous round (18 sts).

Round 8: *4 sc (UK dc), dec 1 st*, rep from * to * twice more (15 sts).

Round 9–11: 1 sc (UK dc) into each st of previous round (15 sts).

Round 12: *3 sc (UK dc), dec 1 st*, rep from * to * twice more (12 sts).

Round 13–16: 1 sc (UK dc) into each st of previous round (12 sts).

Round 17: *2 sc (UK dc), dec 1 st*, rep from * to * twice more (19 sts).

Rounds 18 and 19: 1 sc (UK dc) into each st of previous round (9 sts).

Secure the yarn and fasten off. Do not stuff the ear.

EYES (MAKE 2)

Work in rounds. At the end of each round, work 1 sl st into first st in round, 1 ch, do not turn the work.

Round 1: using Black yarn, work 6 sc (UK dc) into a magic ring (6 sts).

Change to Green yarn.

Round 2: work into the back bar of the stitch only: inc 1 st six times (12 sts). Secure the yarn and fasten off.

BALL OF WOOL

Work in spiral rounds. This means the rounds are not finished with a sl st, nor do you work a turning ch at the beg of a new round.

Round 1: using Pink yarn, work 6 sc (UK dc) into a magic ring (6 sts).

Round 2: inc 1 st six times (12 sts).

Round 3: *1 sc (UK dc), inc 1 st*, rep from * to * five more times (18 sts).

Rounds 4–6: 1 sc (UK dc) into each st of previous round (18 sts).

Round 7: *1 sc (UK dc), dec 1 st*, rep from * to * five more times (12 sts).

Stuff the ball of wool.

Round 8: dec 1 st six times (6 sts).

Round 9: *skip 1 st, 1 sl st*, rep from * to * twice more (3 sts).

Secure the yarn and fasten off. Wrap Pink yarn around the ball of wool several times, and secure the threads here and there with single stitches so it looks like a real ball of wool.

FINISHING OFF

Hold the head so that the inc of rounds 12–14 are facing upwards, and sew eyes to the sides of the head at rounds 14–18. Embroider two French knots with White yarn onto each eye. Sew the last round of each ear to the sides of the head at rounds 28–30. Sew the last round of the body to the underside of the head using whip stitch. With whip stitch, sew the last round of each arm to the body at round 44. Place the ball of wool in the hands and sew a few stitches between them to secure. Press the last round of each leg together and sew the edge to round 14 of the body using whip stitch.

Linda
THE COW

Linda loves strawberries. Her favourite thing is to spend the day grazing in the meadow and watching the clouds in the sky. She once ate too many strawberries, which turned her spots pink – and they stayed that way.

HEIGHT
★ Approx. 11in (28cm)

MATERIALS
★ Austermann Merino 160 (100% merino wool); 1 ball each of Black 202, White 201, Lollipop 256 and Honey 243, and scraps of Rosa 211 and Kiwi 214; 50g/174yd/160m
★ 2.5mm (B-1/UK 13) crochet hook
★ Toy stuffing
★ Tapestry needle

HEAD
Work in spiral rounds. This means the rounds are not finished with a sl st, nor do you work a turning ch at the beg of a new round.

Round 1: using White yarn, work 6 sc (UK dc) into a magic ring (6 sts).

Round 2: inc 1 st six times (12 sts).

Round 3: *1 sc (UK dc), inc 1 st*, rep from * to * five more times (18 sts).

Round 4: *2 sc (UK dc), inc 1 st*, rep from * to * five more times (24 sts).

Round 5: *3 sc (UK dc), inc 1 st*, rep from * to * five more times (30 sts).

Round 6: *4 sc (UK dc), inc 1 st*, rep from * to * five more times (36 sts).

Round 7: *5 sc (UK dc), inc 1 st*, rep from * to * five more times (42 sts).

Round 8: *6 sc (UK dc), inc 1 st*, rep from * to * five more times (48 sts).

Round 9: *7 sc (UK dc), inc 1 st*, rep from * to * five more times (54 sts).

Round 10: *8 sc (UK dc), inc 1 st*, rep from * to * five more times (60 sts).

Round 11: *9 sc (UK dc), inc 1 st*, rep from * to * five more times (66 sts).

Rounds 12–21: 1 sc (UK dc) into each st of previous round (66 sts).

Change to Black yarn.

Rounds 22–31: 1 sc (UK dc) into each st of previous round (66 sts).

Round 32: *9 sc (UK dc), dec 1 st*, rep from * to * five more times (60 sts).

Round 33: 1 sc (UK dc) into each st of previous round (60 sts).

Round 34: *8 sc (UK dc), dec 1 st*, rep from * to * five more times (54 sts).

Round 35: 1 sc (UK dc) into each st of previous round (54 sts).

Round 36: *7 sc (UK dc), dec 1 st*, rep from * to * five more times (48 sts).

Round 37: *6 sc (UK dc), dec 1 st*, rep from * to * five more times (42 sts).

Round 38: *5 sc (UK dc), dec 1 st*, rep from * to * five more times (36 sts).

Round 39: *4 sc (UK dc), dec 1 st*, rep from * to * five more times (30 sts).

Round 40: *3 sc (UK dc), dec 1 st*, rep from * to * five more times (24 sts).

Round 41: *2 sc (UK dc), dec 1 st*, rep from * to * five more times (18 sts).

Round 42: *1 sc (UK dc), dec 1 st*, rep from * to * five more times (12 sts).

Round 43: dec 1 st six times (6 sts).

Round 44: *skip 1 st, 1 sl st*, rep from * to * twice more (3 sts).

Secure the yarn and fasten off.

MUZZLE
Work in rounds. At the end of each round, work 1 sl st into first st in round, 1 ch and turn.

Round 1: work 9 ch with Rosa yarn, 1 sc (UK dc) into second ch from hook, 1 sc (UK dc) into each of next 6 ch, 3 sc (UK dc) into last ch. Continue working on the other side of the length of ch: 6 sc (UK dc), 2 sc (UK dc) into st with first sc (UK dc) (18 sts).

Round 2: inc 1 st, 6 sc (UK dc), inc 1 st three times, 6 sc (UK dc), inc 1 st twice (24 sts).

Round 3: 1 sc (UK dc), inc 1 st, 7 sc (UK dc), inc 1 st, 1 sc (UK dc), inc 1 st, 1 sc (UK dc), inc 1 st, 7 sc (UK dc), inc 1 st, 1 sc (UK dc), inc 1 st (30 sts).

Round 4: 2 sc (UK dc), inc 1 st, 8 sc (UK dc), inc 1 st, 2 sc (UK dc), inc 1 st, 2 sc (UK dc), inc 1 st, 8 sc (UK dc), inc 1 st, 2 sc (UK dc), inc 1 st (36 sts).

Round 5: 3 sc (UK dc), inc 1 st, 9 sc (UK dc), inc 1 st, 3 sc (UK dc), inc 1 st, 3 sc (UK dc), inc 1 st, 9 sc (UK dc), inc 1 st, 3 sc (UK dc), inc 1 st (42 sts).

Rounds 6–10: 1 sc (UK dc) into each st of previous round (42 sts).

Round 8: *6 sc (UK dc), inc 1 st*, rep from * to * five more times (48 sts).

Round 9: *7 sc (UK dc), inc 1 st*, rep from * to * five more times (54 sts).

Rounds 10–12: 1 sc (UK dc) into each st of previous round (54 sts).

Round 13: 4 sc (UK dc) in White yarn, 7 sc (UK dc) in Lollipop yarn, 13 sc (UK dc) in White yarn, 3 sc (UK dc) in Lollipop yarn, 12 sc (UK dc) in White yarn, 5 sc (UK dc) in Lollipop yarn, 10 sc (UK dc) in White yarn (54 sts).

Round 14: 3 sc (UK dc) in White yarn, 10 sc (UK dc) in Lollipop yarn, 10 sc (UK dc) in White yarn, 5 sc (UK dc) in Lollipop yarn, 11 sc (UK dc) in White yarn, 6 sc (UK dc) in Lollipop yarn, 9 sc (UK dc) in White yarn (54 sts).

Round 15: 3 sc (UK dc) in White yarn, 12 sc (UK dc) in Lollipop yarn, 8 sc (UK dc) in White yarn, 6 sc (UK dc) in Lollipop yarn, 10 sc (UK dc) in White yarn, 7 sc (UK dc) in Lollipop yarn, 8 sc (UK dc) in White yarn (54 sts).

Round 16: 3 sc (UK dc) in White yarn, 11 sc (UK dc) in Lollipop yarn, 8 sc (UK dc) in White yarn, 8 sc (UK dc) in Lollipop yarn, 10 sc (UK dc) in White yarn, 6 sc (UK dc) in Lollipop yarn, 8 sc (UK dc) in White yarn (54 sts).

Round 17: 4 sc (UK dc) in White yarn, 9 sc (UK dc) in Lollipop yarn, 9 sc (UK dc) in White yarn, 6 sc (UK dc) in Lollipop yarn, 13 sc (UK dc) in White yarn, 3 sc (UK dc) in Lollipop yarn, 5 sc (UK dc) in White yarn, 4 sc (UK dc) in Lollipop yarn, 1 sc (UK dc) in White yarn (54 sts).

Round 18: 3 sc (UK dc) in White yarn, 8 sc (UK dc) in Lollipop yarn, 6 sc (UK dc) in White yarn, 2 sc (UK dc) in Lollipop yarn, 4 sc (UK dc) in White yarn, 6 sc (UK dc) in Lollipop yarn, 5 sc (UK dc) in White yarn, 2 sc (UK dc) in Lollipop yarn, 6 sc (UK dc) in White yarn, 2 sc (UK dc) in Lollipop yarn, 5 sc (UK dc) in White yarn, 5 sc (UK dc) in Lollipop yarn (54 sts).

Round 19: 5 sc (UK dc) in White yarn, 6 sc (UK dc) in Lollipop yarn, 5 sc (UK dc) in White yarn, 4 sc (UK dc) in Lollipop yarn, 5 sc (UK dc) in White yarn, 3 sc (UK dc) in Lollipop yarn, 5 sc (UK dc) in White yarn, 5 sc (UK dc) in Lollipop yarn, 12 sc (UK dc) in White yarn, 3 sc (UK dc) in Lollipop yarn, 1 sc (UK dc) in White yarn (54 sts).

Round 20: 7 sc (UK dc) in White yarn, 3 sc (UK dc) in Lollipop yarn, 6 sc (UK dc) in White yarn, 4 sc (UK dc) in Lollipop yarn, 13 sc (UK dc) in White yarn, 6 sc (UK dc) in Lollipop yarn, 15 sc (UK dc) in White yarn (54 sts).

Round 21: 16 sc (UK dc) in White yarn, 5 sc (UK dc) in Lollipop yarn, 12 sc (UK dc) in White yarn, 6 sc (UK dc) in Lollipop yarn, 7 sc (UK dc) in White yarn, 2 sc (UK dc) in Lollipop yarn, 6 sc (UK dc) in White yarn (54 sts).

Round 22: 15 sc (UK dc) in White yarn, 5 sc (UK dc) in Lollipop yarn, 14 sc (UK dc) in White yarn, 5 sc (UK dc) in Lollipop yarn, 6 sc (UK dc) in White yarn, 4 sc (UK dc) in Lollipop yarn, 5 sc (UK dc) in White yarn (54 sts).

Round 23: 1 sc (UK dc) in White yarn, 3 sc (UK dc) in Lollipop yarn, 12 sc (UK dc) in White yarn, 4 sc (UK dc) in Lollipop yarn, 5 sc (UK dc) in White yarn, 3 sc (UK dc) in Lollipop yarn, 6 sc (UK dc) in White yarn, 4 sc (UK dc) in Lollipop yarn, 5 sc (UK dc) in White yarn, 6 sc (UK dc) in Lollipop yarn, 5 sc (UK dc) in White yarn (54 sts).

Round 24: 1 sc (UK dc) in White yarn, 4 sc (UK dc) in Lollipop yarn, 11 sc (UK dc) in White yarn, 5 sc (UK dc) in Lollipop yarn, 4 sc (UK dc) in White yarn, 4 sc (UK dc) in Lollipop yarn, 5 sc (UK dc) in White yarn, 3 sc (UK dc) in Lollipop yarn, 7 sc (UK dc) in White yarn, 4 sc (UK dc) in Lollipop yarn, 6 sc (UK dc) in White yarn (54 sts).

Round 25: 1 sc (UK dc) in White yarn, 5 sc (UK dc) in Lollipop yarn, 12 sc (UK dc) in White yarn, 5 sc (UK dc) in Lollipop yarn, 12 sc (UK dc) in White yarn, 3 sc (UK dc) in Lollipop yarn, 8 sc (UK dc) in White yarn, 2 sc (UK dc) in Lollipop yarn, 6 sc (UK dc) in White yarn (54 sts).

Round 11: 4 sc (UK dc), inc 1 st, 10 sc (UK dc), inc 1 st, 4 sc (UK dc), inc 1 st, 4 sc (UK dc), inc 1 st, 10 sc (UK dc), inc 1 st, 4 sc (UK dc), inc 1 st (48 sts).

Rounds 12 and 13: 1 sc (UK dc) into each st of previous round (48 sts). Secure the yarn and fasten off, leaving a long tail.

BODY

Work in rounds. At the end of each round, work 1 sl st into first st in round, 1 ch and turn. For the cow's marks, the colours frequently change within a round. Crochet around the yarn not currently being used.

Round 1: using White yarn, work 6 sc (UK dc) into a magic ring (6 sts).

Round 2: inc 1 st six times (12 sts).

Round 3: *1 sc (UK dc), inc 1 st*, rep from * to * five more times (18 sts).

Round 4: *2 sc (UK dc), inc 1 st*, rep from * to * five more times (24 sts).

Round 5: *3 sc (UK dc), inc 1 st*, rep from * to * five more times (30 sts).

Round 6: *4 sc (UK dc), inc 1 st*, rep from * to * five more times (36 sts).

Round 7: *5 sc (UK dc), inc 1 st*, rep from * to * five more times (42 sts).

Round 26: 1 sc (UK dc) in White yarn, 4 sc (UK dc) in Lollipop yarn, 10 sc (UK dc) in White yarn, 7 sc (UK dc) in Lollipop yarn, 13 sc (UK dc) in White yarn, 5 sc (UK dc) in Lollipop yarn, 14 sc (UK dc) in White yarn (54 sts).

Round 27: 2 sc (UK dc) in White yarn, 3 sc (UK dc) in Lollipop yarn, 4 sc (UK dc) in White yarn, 3 sc (UK dc) in Lollipop yarn, 5 sc (UK dc) in White yarn, 3 sc (UK dc) in Lollipop yarn, 34 sc (UK dc) in White yarn (54 sts).

Round 28: 8 sc (UK dc) in White yarn, 5 sc (UK dc) in Lollipop yarn, 15 sc (UK dc) in White yarn, 4 sc (UK dc) in Lollipop yarn, 22 sc (UK dc) in White yarn (54 sts).

Round 29: 7 sc (UK dc) in White yarn, 7 sc (UK dc) in Lollipop yarn, 14 sc (UK dc) in White yarn, 5 sc (UK dc) in Lollipop yarn, 21 sc (UK dc) in White yarn (54 sts).

Round 30: 7 sc (UK dc) in White yarn, dec 1 st, 7 sc (UK dc) in Lollipop yarn, 1 sc (UK dc) dec 1 st, 6 sc (UK dc), dec 1 st, 1 sc (UK dc) in White yarn, 5 sc (UK dc) in Lollipop yarn, 1 sc (UK dc), dec 1 st, 7 sc (UK dc), dec 1 st, 7 sc (UK dc), dec 1 st in White yarn (48 sts).

Round 31: 5 sc (UK dc), dec 1 st in White yarn, 7 sc (UK dc) in Lollipop yarn, dec 1 st, 6 sc (UK dc), dec 1 st, 1 sc (UK dc) in White yarn, 5 sc (UK dc) in Lollipop yarn, dec 1 st, 6 sc (UK dc), dec 1 st, 1 sc (UK dc) in White yarn, 4 sc (UK dc) in Lollipop yarn, 1 sc (UK dc), dec 1 st in White yarn (42 sts).

Round 32: 4 sc (UK dc), dec 1 st in White yarn, 5 sc (UK dc) in Lollipop yarn, 1 sc (UK dc), dec 1 st, 5 sc (UK dc), dec 1 st, 3 sc (UK dc) in White yarn, 2 sc (UK dc) in Lollipop yarn, dec 1 st, 5 sc (UK dc), dec 1 st, 1 sc (UK dc) in White yarn, 4 sc (UK dc) in Lollipop yarn, dec 1 st in White yarn (36 sts).

Work the last round with only White yarn.

Round 33: *4 sc (UK dc), dec 1 st*, rep from * to * five more times (30 sts).

Secure the yarn and leave a long tail. Stuff the body.

EARS (MAKE 2)

Work in rounds. At the end of each round, work 1 sl st into first st in round, 1 ch and turn.

Round 1: using Black yarn, work 3 sc (UK dc) into a magic ring (3 sts).

Round 2: inc 1 st three times (6 sts).

Round 3: 1 sc (UK dc) into each st of previous round (6 sts).

Round 4: *1 sc (UK dc), inc 1 st*, rep from * to * twice more (9 sts).

Round 5: *2 sc (UK dc), inc 1 st*, rep from * to * twice more (12 sts).

Round 6: 1 sc (UK dc) into each st of previous round (12 sts).

Round 7: *3 sc (UK dc), inc 1 st*, rep from * to * twice more (15 sts).

Round 8: *4 sc (UK dc), inc 1 st*, rep from * to * twice more (18 sts).

Round 9: *5 sc (UK dc), inc 1 st*, rep from * to * twice more (21 sts).

Rounds 10–16: 1 sc (UK dc) into each st of previous round (21 sts).

Round 17: *5 sc (UK dc), dec 1 st*, rep from * to * twice more (18 sts).

Round 18: *4 sc (UK dc), dec 1 st*, rep from * to * twice more (15 sts).

Round 19: *3 sc (UK dc), dec 1 st*, rep from * to * twice more (12 sts).

Round 20: *2 sc (UK dc), dec 1 st*, rep from * to * twice more (9 sts).

Round 21: *1 sc (UK dc), dec 1 st* rep from * to * twice more (6 sts).

Round 22: *skip 1 st, 1 sc (UK dc)*, rep from * to * twice more (3 sts).

Secure the yarn and fasten off. Do not stuff the ear.

HORNS (MAKE 2)

Work in spiral rounds. This means the rounds are not finished with a sl st, nor do you work a turning ch at the beg of a new round.

Round 1: using Honey yarn, work 3 sc (UK dc) into a magic ring (3 sts).

Round 2: inc 1 st three times (6 sts).

Round 3: 1 sc (UK dc) into each st of previous round (6 sts).

Round 4: *1 sc (UK dc), inc 1 st*, rep from * to * twice more (9 sts).

Round 5: 1 sc (UK dc) into each st of previous round (9 sts).

Round 6: *2 sc (UK dc), inc 1 st*, rep from * to * twice more (12 sts).

Round 7: 1 sc (UK dc) into each st of previous round (12 sts).

Round 8: *3 sc (UK dc), inc 1 st*, rep from * to * twice more (15 sts).

Round 9: 1 sc (UK dc) into each st of previous round (15 sts).

Secure the yarn and fasten off. Loosely stuff the horn.

ARMS (MAKE 2)

Work in spiral rounds. This means the rounds are not finished with a sl st, nor do you work a turning ch at the beg of a new round.

Round 1: using Honey yarn, work 6 sc (UK dc) into a magic ring (6 sts).

Round 2: inc 1 st six times (12 sts).

Rounds 3–6: 1 sc (UK dc) into each st of previous round (12 sts).

Change to White yarn.

Rounds 7–25: 1 sc (UK dc) into each st of previous round (12 sts).

Secure the yarn and fasten off. Stuff the arm loosely.

LEGS (MAKE 2)

Work in spiral rounds. This means the rounds are not finished with a sl st, nor do you work a turning ch at the beg of a new round.

Round 1: using Honey yarn, work 6 sc (UK dc) into a magic ring (6 sts).

Round 2: inc 1 st six times (12 sts).

Round 3: *1 sc (UK dc), inc 1 st*, rep from * to * five more times (18 sts).

Round 4: *2 sc (UK dc), inc 1 st*, rep from * to * five more times (24 sts).

Rounds 5–8: 1 sc (UK dc) into each st of previous round (24 sts).

Round 9: *2 sc (UK dc), dec 1 st*, rep from * to * five more times (18 sts).

Round 10: dec 1 st six times, 6 sc (UK dc) (12 sts).

Change to White yarn.

Rounds 11–18: 1 sc (UK dc) into each st of previous round (12 sts).

Round 19: *1 sc (UK dc), inc 1 st*, rep from * to * five more times (18 sts).

Rounds 20 and 21: 1 sc (UK dc) into each st of previous round (18 sts).

Round 22: *2 sc (UK dc), inc 1 st*, rep from * to * five more times (24 sts).

Stuff the leg to this point.

Rounds 23 and 24: 1 sc (UK dc) into each st of previous round (24 sts).

Round 25: *2 sc (UK dc), dec 1 st*, rep from * to * five more times (18 sts).

Round 26: *1 sc (UK dc), dec 1 st*, rep from * to * five more times (12 sts).

Round 27: dec 1 st six times (6 sts).

Secure the yarn and fasten off.

UDDER

Work in spiral rounds.

Round 1: using Rosa yarn, work 6 sc (UK dc) into a magic ring (6 sts).

Round 2: inc 1 st six times (12 sts).

Round 3: *1 sc (UK dc), inc 1 st*, rep from * to * five more times (18 sts).

Round 4: *2 sc (UK dc), inc 1 st, 2 ch, skip 2 sts, inc 1 st, 2 ch, skip 2 sts, inc 1 st*, rep from * to * once more (24 sts).

Round 5: *3 sc (UK dc), inc 1 st*, rep from * to * five more times (30 sts).

Rounds 6–8: 1 sc (UK dc) into each st of previous round (30 sts).

Secure the yarn and fasten off.

NIPPLES (MAKE 4)

Work in spiral rounds.

Round 1: using Rosa yarn, work 6 sc (UK dc) into a magic ring (6 sts).

Rounds 2–4: 1 sc (UK dc) into each st of previous round (6 sts).

Secure the yarn and fasten off. Do not stuff.

TAIL

Work in spiral rounds.

Round 1: using White yarn, work 6 sc (UK dc) into a magic ring (6 sts).

Rounds 2–18: 1 sc (UK dc) into each st of previous round (6 sts).

Secure the yarn and fasten off. Join Black yarn to the magic ring and work as follows: 3 ch, 1 sl st into the magic ring, 3 ch, 1 sl st into the magic ring.

Secure the yarn and fasten off.

EYES (MAKE 2)

Work in rounds. Work 1 ch to turn at the beg of each round, and finish each round with 1 sl st in the first st of the round.

Round 1: using Black yarn, work 6 sc (UK dc) into a magic ring (6 sts). Change to Kiwi yarn.

Round 2: work into the back bar of the stitch only: inc 1 st six times (12 sts).

Secure the yarn and fasten off.

FINISHING OFF

Using whip stitch, sew the last round of the body to the first round of the head and sew the arms to the last round of the body. Sew the udder to the front of the body at rounds 2–12 and attach the nipples evenly. For each leg, press the last round together and sew the edge to rounds 12–15 at the side of the body. To shape the hoof, use a tapestry needle and Honey yarn and sew between the magic ring for the leg and the third dec of round 10. Pull the yarn tight and secure with a little knot. Sew the muzzle to the front lower half of the head, then sew the eyes above the muzzle on the black area of the head. With White yarn, embroider two French knots onto the pupils. Using whip stitch, sew the horns to the upper part of the head. Sew the ears below the horns.

Priscilla
THE PIG

Priscilla loves to dance. Anytime, anywhere, any dance! Her favourites are grooving along to Latin American beats, pirouetting in ballets and experimenting with modern dance.

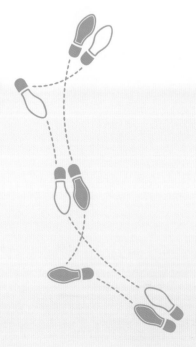

HEIGHT
★ Approx. 12½in (32cm)

MATERIAL
★ Lang Yarns Kappa (97% cotton, 3% polyester); 1 ball of Rosa 0019; 50g/137yd/125m
★ Lang Yarns Kappa Color (97% cotton, 3% polyester); 1 ball of Salmon/Turquoise 0228; 50g/137yd/125m
★ Austermann Merino 160 (100% merino wool); scraps of Black 202 and White 201; 50g/174yd/160m
★ 2.5mm (B-1/UK 13) crochet hook
★ Toy stuffing
★ Tapestry needle

HEAD
Work in spiral rounds. This means the rounds are not finished with a sl st, nor do you work a turning ch at the beg of a new round.

Round 1: using Rosa yarn, work 6 sc (UK dc) into a magic ring (6 sts).
Round 2: inc 1 st six times (12 sts).
Round 3: *1 sc (UK dc), inc 1 st*, rep from * to * five more times (18 sts).
Round 4: *2 sc (UK dc), inc 1 st*, rep from * to * five more times (24 sts).
Round 5: *3 sc (UK dc), inc 1 st*, rep from * to * five more times (30 sts).
Rounds 6 and 7: 1 sc (UK dc) into each st of previous round (30 sts).
Round 8: *4 sc (UK dc), inc 1 st*, rep from * to * five more times (36 sts).
Rounds 9 and 10: 1 sc (UK dc) into each st of previous round (36 sts).
Round 11: *5 sc (UK dc), inc 1 st*, rep from * to * five more times (42 sts).
Rounds 12 and 13: 1 sc (UK dc) into each st of previous round (42 sts).
Round 14: *6 sc (UK dc), inc 1 st*, rep from * to * twice more, *5 sc (UK dc), dec 1 st*, rep from * to * twice more (42 sts).

Round 15: *7 sc (UK dc), inc 1 st*, rep from * to * twice more, 18 sc (UK dc) (45 sts).
Round 16: *8 sc (UK dc), inc 1 st*, rep from * to * twice more, 18 sc (UK dc) (48 sts).
Round 17: 1 sc (UK dc) into each st of previous round (48 sts).
Round 18: *9 sc (UK dc), inc 1 st*, rep from * to * twice more, *4 sc (UK dc), dec 1 st* rep from * to * twice more (48 sts).
Rounds 19–24: 1 sc (UK dc) into each st of previous round (48 sts).
Round 25: *6 sc (UK dc), dec 1 st*, rep from * to * five more times (42 sts).
Round 26: *5 sc (UK dc), dec 1 st*, rep from * to * five more times (36 sts).
Stuff the head.
Round 27: *4 sc (UK dc), dec 1 st*, rep from * to * five more times (30 sts).
Round 28: *3 sc (UK dc), dec 1 st*, rep from * to * five more times (24 sts).
Round 29: *2 sc (UK dc), dec 1 st*, rep from * to * five more times (18 sts).

Round 30: *1 sc (UK dc), dec 1 st*, rep from * to * five more times (12 sts).
Round 31: dec 1 st six times (6 sts).
Round 32: *skip 1 st, 1 sl st*, rep from * to * twice more (3 sts).
Secure the yarn and fasten off.

BODY
Work in spiral rounds. This means the rounds are not finished with a sl st, nor do you work a turning ch at the beg of a new round.

Round 1: using Salmon/Turquoise yarn, work 6 sc (UK dc) into a magic ring (6 sts).
Round 2: inc 1 st six times (12 sts).
Round 3: *1 sc (UK dc), inc 1 st*, rep from * to * five more times (18 sts).
Round 4: *2 sc (UK dc), inc 1 st*, rep from * to * five more times (24 sts).
Rounds 5–7: 1 sc (UK dc) into each st of previous round (24 sts).
Round 8: *3 sc (UK dc), inc 1 st*, rep from * to * five more times (30 sts).

Rounds 9–11: 1 sc (UK dc) into each st of previous round (30 sts).

Round 12: *4 sc (UK dc), inc 1 st*, rep from * to * five more times (36 sts).

Rounds 13–15: 1 sc (UK dc) into each st of previous round (36 sts).

Round 16: *5 sc (UK dc), inc 1 st*, rep from * to * five more times (42 sts).

Rounds 17–19: 1 sc (UK dc) into each st of previous round (42 sts).

Round 20: *6 sc (UK dc), inc 1 st*, rep from * to * five more times (48 sts).

Rounds 21–23: 1 sc (UK dc) into each st of previous round (48 sts).

Round 24: *7 sc (UK dc), inc 1 st*, rep from * to * five more times (54 sts).

Round 25: 1 sc (UK dc) into each st of previous round (54 sts).

Now work as follows for the skirt:

Round 26: work into the front bar of the stitch only: *2 sc (UK dc), inc 1 st*, rep from * to * 17 more times (72 sts).

Round 27: 1 sc (UK dc) into each st of previous round (72 sts).

Round 28: *2 dc (UK tr), 2 dc (UK tr) in 1 st*, rep from * to * twenty-three more times (96 sts).

Round 29: work 2 hdc (UK htr) into each st of previous round (192 sts).

Secure the yarn and fasten off. Join Rosa yarn to the back bar of the first st of round 25, and finish the body as follows:

Round 26: work into the back bar of the stitch only: 1 sc (UK dc) in each st of previous round (54 sts).

Round 27: *8 sc (UK dc), inc 1 st*, rep from * to * five more times (60 sts).

Rounds 28–30: 1 sc (UK dc) into each st of previous round (60 sts).

Round 31: *8 sc (UK dc), dec 1 st*, rep from * to * five more times (54 sts).

Round 32: *7 sc (UK dc), dec 1 st*, rep from * to * five more times (48 sts).

Round 33: *6 sc (UK dc), dec 1 st*, rep from * to * five more times (42 sts).

Round 34: *5 sc (UK dc), dec 1 st*, rep from * to * five more times (36 sts).

Stuff the body.

Round 35: *4 sc (UK dc), dec 1 st*, rep from * to * five more times (30 sts).

Round 36: *3 sc (UK dc), dec 1 st*, rep from * to * five more times (24 sts).

Round 37: *2 sc (UK dc), dec 1 st*, rep from * to * five more times (18 sts).

Round 38: *1 sc (UK dc), dec 1 st*, rep from * to * five more times (12 sts).

Round 39: dec 1 st six times (6 sts).

Round 40: *skip 1 st, 1 sl st*, rep from * to * twice more (3 sts).

Secure the yarn and fasten off.

LEGS (MAKE 2)

Work in spiral rounds. This means the rounds are not finished with a sl st, nor do you work a turning ch at the beg of a new round.

Round 1: using Rosa yarn, work 6 sc (UK dc) into a magic ring (6 sts).

Round 2: inc 1 st six times (12 sts).

Round 3: work into the back bar of the stitch only: 1 sc (UK dc) into each st of previous round (12 sts).

Rounds 4–27: 1 sc (UK dc) into each st of previous round (12 sts).

Round 28: inc 1 st three times, 9 sc (UK dc) (15 sts).

Round 29: *1 sc (UK dc), inc 1 st*, rep from * to * twice more, 9 sc (UK dc) (18 sts).

Round 30: *2 sc (UK dc), inc 1 st*, rep from * to * twice more, 9 sc (UK dc) (21 sts).

Round 31: *3 sc (UK dc), inc 1 st*, rep from * to * twice more, 9 sc (UK dc) (24 sts).

Rounds 32–35: 1 sc (UK dc) into each st of previous round (24 sts).

Secure the yarn and fasten off. Stuff the leg.

ARMS (MAKE 2)

Work in spiral rounds. This means the rounds are not finished with a sl st, nor do you work a turning ch at the beg of a new round.

Round 1: using Rosa yarn, work 6 sc (UK dc) into a magic ring (6 sts).

Rounds 2–22: 1 sc (UK dc) into each st of previous round (6 sts).

Change to Salmon/Turquoise yarn.

Rounds 23–30: 1 sc (UK dc) into each st of previous round (6 sts).

Secure the yarn and fasten off. Do not stuff the arm.

EARS (MAKE 2)

Work in rounds. At the end of each round, work 1 sl st into first st in round, 1 ch and turn.

Round 1: using Rosa yarn, work 6 sc (UK dc) into a magic ring (6 sts).

Round 2: 1 sc (UK dc) into each st of previous round (6 sts).

Round 3: *1 sc (UK dc), inc 1 st*, rep from * to * twice more (9 sts).

Round 4: 1 sc (UK dc) into each st of previous round (9 sts).

Round 5: *2 sc (UK dc), inc 1 st*, rep from * to * twice more (12 sts).

Round 6: 1 sc (UK dc) into each st of previous round (12 sts).

Round 7: *1 sc (UK dc), inc 1 st*, rep from * to * five more times (18 sts).

Rounds 8–10: 1 sc (UK dc) into each st of previous round (18 sts).

Round 11: *1 sc (UK dc), dec 1 st*, rep from * to * five more times (12 sts).

Secure the yarn and fasten off. Do not stuff the ear.

CURLY TAIL

Row 1: using Rosa yarn, work 20 ch, 2 sc (UK dc) into second ch from hook. 2 sc (UK dc) into each remaining ch (38 sts). Secure the yarn and fasten off.

EYES (MAKE 2)

Round 1: using Black yarn, work 6 sc (UK dc) into a magic ring (6 sts).

Join in a round with sl st into the first st. Secure the yarn and fasten off.

FINISHING OFF

When weaving in the yarn from the magic ring for the head, pull the yarn tight into the head to make a pig's snout. Secure with a little knot and conceal it. Sew the eyes to the head. Using White yarn, embroider two French knots on each eye. Sew two eyelashes beside each eye using Black yarn. Press the last round of each ear together and sew the edge to the side of the head using whip stitch. Sew the first round of the body to the underside of the head. Attach the curly tail to the back, below the skirt. Press the last round of each arm together, and sew to the sides of the body using whip stitch. Press the last round of each leg together, and sew to the sides of the body below the skirt using whip stitch. Secure the thighs against the body with a few hidden stitches. To shape the hoof, use a tapestry needle and attach Rosa yarn at the back of round 7 of the leg. Pull across the magic ring and insert in front of the leg at round 7 and pull yarn tight. Secure with a little knot and conceal it.

Clara
THE CAT

Clara is the fastest cat around and a champion mouser. To keep up with those speedy mice she needs the right footwear. She's lightning fast in her lucky blue boots! Better watch out, mice!

HEIGHT

★ Approx. 15¾in (40cm)

MATERIALS

★ Austermann Merino 160 (100% merino wool); 2 balls of Kiwi 214, 1 ball of Jeans 223, and scraps of Natur 210, Black 202, Petrol 233 and Rosa 211; 50g/174yd/160m
★ 2.5mm (B-1/UK 13) crochet hook
★ Toy stuffing
★ Tapestry needle

HEAD

Work in spiral rounds. This means the rounds are not finished with a sl st, nor do you work a turning ch at the beg of a new round.

Round 1: using Kiwi yarn, work 6 sc (UK dc) into a magic ring (6 sts).

Round 2: inc 1 st six times (12 sts).

Round 3: *1 sc (UK dc), inc 1 st*, rep from * to * five more times (18 sts).

Round 4: *2 sc (UK dc), inc 1 st*, rep from * to * five more times (24 sts).

Round 5: *3 sc (UK dc), inc 1 st*, rep from * to * five more times (30 sts).

Round 6: *4 sc (UK dc), inc 1 st*, rep from * to * five more times (36 sts).

Round 7: *5 sc (UK dc), inc 1 st*, rep from * to * five more times (42 sts).

Round 8: *6 sc (UK dc), inc 1 st*, rep from * to * five more times (48 sts).

Round 9: *7 sc (UK dc), inc 1 st*, rep from * to * five more times (54 sts).

Round 10: *8 sc (UK dc), inc 1 st*, rep from * to * five more times (60 sts).

Round 11: *9 sc (UK dc), inc 1 st*, rep from * to * five more times (66 sts).

Round 12: *10 sc (UK dc), inc 1 st*, rep from * to * five more times (72 sts).

Rounds 13–24: 1 sc (UK dc) into each st of previous round (72 sts).

Round 25: *10 sc (UK dc), dec 1 st*, rep from * to * five more times (66 sts).

Rounds 26–28: 1 sc (UK dc) into each st of previous round (66 sts).

Round 29: 18 sc (UK dc), skip 48 sts (18 sts).

Work the first st of the next round in the first st of the previous round as usual.

Round 30: 1 sc (UK dc) into each st of previous round (18 sts).

Round 31: *4 sc (UK dc), dec 1 st*, rep from * to * twice more (15 sts).

Round 32: 1 sc (UK dc) into each st of previous round (15 sts).

Round 33: dec 1 st, 11 sc (UK dc), dec 1 st (13 sts).

Round 34: dec 1 st, 9 sc (UK dc), dec 1 st (11 sts).

Round 35: dec 1 st, 7 sc (UK dc), dec 1 st (9 sts).

Round 36: *1 sc (UK dc), dec 1 st*, rep from * to * twice more (6 sts).

Round 37: 1 sc (UK dc) into each st of previous round (6 sts).

Round 38: *skip 1 st, 1 sl st*, rep from * to * twice more (3 sts).

Secure the yarn and fasten off. Go back to round 29, skip 15 sts after the 18 sts already crocheted, join Kiwi yarn to 34th st of round 29, and continue crocheting as follows:

Round 29: 18 sc (UK dc), do not work the remaining 15 sts (18 sts).

Work the first st of the next round in the first st of the previous round as usual.

Round 30: 13 sc (UK dc), dec 1 st, 3 sc (UK dc) (17 sts).

Round 31: 1 sc (UK dc), dec 1 st, 4 sc (UK dc), dec 1 st, 8 sc (UK dc) (15 sts).

Round 32: 13 sc (UK dc), dec 1 st (14 sts).

Round 33: dec 1 st, 10 sc (UK dc), dec 1 st (12 sts).

Round 34: dec 1 st, 8 sc (UK dc), dec 1 st (10 sts).

Round 35: dec 1 st, 4 sc (UK dc), dec 1 st, 2 sc (UK dc) (8 sts).

Round 36: dec 1 st, 1 sc (UK dc), dec 1 st, 3 sc (UK dc) (6 sts).

Round 37: 1 sc (UK dc) into each st of previous round (6 sts).

Round 38: *skip 1 st, 1 sl st*, rep from to * twice more (3 sts).

Secure the yarn and fasten off.

Stuff the head. Sew up the opening between the ears using whip stitch.

BODY

Work in spiral rounds. This means the rounds are not finished with a sl st, nor do you work a turning ch at the beg of a new round.

Round 1: using Kiwi yarn, work 6 sc (UK dc) into a magic ring (6 sts).

Round 2: inc 1 st six times (12 sts).

Round 3: *1 sc (UK dc), inc 1 st*, rep from * to * five more times (18 sts).

Round 4: *2 sc (UK dc), inc 1 st*, rep from * to * five more times (24 sts).

Round 5: *3 sc (UK dc), inc 1 st*, rep from * to * five more times (30 sts).

Round 6: *4 sc (UK dc), inc 1 st*, rep from * to * five more times (36 sts).

Round 7: *5 sc (UK dc), inc 1 st*, rep from * to * five more times (42 sts).

Round 8: *6 sc (UK dc), inc 1 st*, rep from * to * five more times (48 sts).

Round 9: *7 sc (UK dc), inc 1 st*, rep from * to * five more times (54 sts).

Rounds 10–17: 1 sc (UK dc) into each st of previous round (54 sts).

Round 18: *7 sc (UK dc), dec 1 st*, rep from * to * five more times (48 sts).

Rounds 19–31: 1 sc (UK dc) into each st of previous round (48 sts).

Round 32: *6 sc (UK dc), dec 1 st*, rep from * to * five more times (42 sts).

Rounds 33–43: 1 sc (UK dc) into each st of previous round (42 sts).

Stuff the body.

Round 44: *5 sc (UK dc), dec 1 st*, rep from * to * five more times (36 sts).

Round 45: *4 sc (UK dc), dec 1 st*, rep from * to * five more times (30 sts).

Round 46: *3 sc (UK dc), dec 1 st*, rep from * to * five more times (24 sts).

Secure the yarn and fasten off.

ARMS (MAKE 2)

Work in spiral rounds. This means the rounds are not finished with a sl st, nor do you work a turning ch at the beg of a new round.

Round 1: using Kiwi yarn, work 6 sc (UK dc) into a magic ring (6 sts).

Round 2: inc 1 st six times (12 sts).

Round 3: *1 sc (UK dc), inc 1 st*, rep from * to * five more times (18 sts).

Round 4: *2 sc (UK dc), inc 1 st*, rep from * to * five more times (24 sts).

Rounds 5–7: 1 sc (UK dc) into each st of previous round (24 sts).

Round 8: *2 sc (UK dc), dec 1 st*, rep from * to * five more times (18 sts).

Rounds 9–37: 1 sc (UK dc) into each st of previous round (18 sts).

Secure the yarn and fasten off.

Rounds 1–11 make the cat's paw, and are not stuffed. Sew a few stitches along round 11 to divide the hand and arm. Stuff the arm from round 12, stuffing the top of the arm loosely. Press the hand so it bends slightly, and secure with a few stitches.

LEGS (MAKE 2)

Start off working in rounds. At the end of each round, work 1 sl st into first st in round, 1 ch and turn.

Round 1: using Jeans yarn, work 7 ch, 1 sc (UK dc) into second ch from hook, 1 sc (UK dc) into each of next 4 ch, 3 sc (UK dc) into last ch. Continue working on the other side of the length of ch: 4 sc (UK dc), 2 sc (UK dc) into same st as the first st (14 sts).

Round 2: inc 1 st, 4 sc (UK dc), inc 1 st three times, 4 sc (UK dc), inc 1 st twice (20 sts).

Round 3: 1 sc (UK dc), inc 1 st, 5 sc (UK dc), inc 1 st, 1 sc (UK dc), inc 1 st, 1 sc (UK dc), inc 1 st, 5 sc (UK dc), inc 1 st, 1 sc (UK dc), inc 1 st (26 sts).

Round 4: work into the back bar of the stitch only: 1 sc (UK dc) into each st of previous round (26 sts).

Rounds 5 and 6: 1 sc (UK dc) into each st of previous round (26 sts).

Round 7: 5 sc (UK dc), dec 1 st seven times, 7 sc (UK dc) (19 sts).

Round 8: 1 sc (UK dc) into each st of previous round (19 sts).

Round 9: 4 sc (UK dc), dec 1 st twice, skip 1 st, dec 1 st twice, 6 sc (UK dc) (14 sts).

Rounds 10–21: 1 sc (UK dc) into each st of previous round (14 sts).

Round 22: work into the front bar of the stitch only. * 6 sc (UK dc), inc 1 st *, rep from * to * once (16 sts).

Round 23: *3 sc (UK dc), inc 1 st*, rep from * to * three more times (20 sts).

Round 24: *4 sc (UK dc), inc 1 st*, rep from * to * three more times (24 sts).

Secure the yarn and fasten off.

Join Kiwi yarn to the back bar of the first st of round 22, and crochet as follows in spiral rounds:

Rounds 23–46: 1 sc (UK dc) into each st of previous round (24 sts).

Secure yarn and fasten off. Stuff the leg.

EYES (MAKE 2)

Work in rounds. At the end of each round, work 1 sl st into first st in round, 1 ch and turn.

Round 1: using Black yarn, work 6 sc (UK dc) into a magic ring (6 sts).

Round 2: inc 1 st six times (12 sts).
Change to Petrol yarn.

Round 3: work into the back bar of the stitch only: *1 sc (UK dc), inc 1 st*, rep from * to * five more times (18 sts).
Secure the yarn and fasten off.

MOUTH

Work in rounds. At the end of each round, work 1 sl st into first st in round, 1 ch and turn.

Round 1: using Natur yarn, work 8 ch, 1 sc (UK dc) into second ch from hook, 1 sc (UK dc) into each of next 6 ch, 3 sc

(UK dc) into last ch. Continue working on the other side of the length of ch: 6 sc (UK dc), 2 sc (UK dc) into ch with first st in (18 sts).

Round 2: inc 1 st, 6 sc (UK dc), inc 1 st three times, 6 sc (UK dc), inc 1 st twice (24 sts).

Round 3: 1 sc (UK dc), inc 1 st, 2 hdc (UK htr) in 1 st, 4 dc (UK tr), 2 hdc (UK htr) in 1 st, inc 1 st, 15 sc (UK dc) (28 sts).

Rounds 4 and 5: 1 sc (UK dc) into each st of previous round (28 sts).
Secure the yarn and fasten off.

TAIL

Work in spiral rounds. This means the rounds are not finished with a sl st, nor do you work a turning ch at the beg of a new round.

Round 1: using Kiwi yarn, work 6 sc (UK dc) into a magic ring (6 sts).
Work 1 sc (UK dc) into each st of the previous round until your work measures 5½in (14cm).

FINISHING OFF

Sew the last round of the body to the underside of the head. Press the last round of each arm together, and sew the edge to the side of the body at round 44 using whip stitch. Make sure that the palms are facing the body. Sew the last round of each leg to the underside of the body using whip stitch. Sew the last round of the tail to the back of the body.

Backstitch the last round of the eyes to the head. Embroider two French knots in White yarn onto each eye. With Black yarn, sew two eyelashes to each eye coming from the pupil. Sew the last round of the mouth to the head below the eyes, and stuff before sewing up. Using Rosa yarn, sew a few horizontal stitches to the top of the mouth for the nose.

Babs
THE BEE

Babs loves everything about the summer! She particularly likes the colourful window boxes in the city, where she works gathering nectar for her family.

HEIGHT

★ Approx. 11¾in (30cm)

MATERIALS

★ Lana Grossa Wakame (75% cotton, 25% synthetic); 1 ball each of Black 09, Yellow 10 and White 01, and scraps of Pink 13; 50g/136yd/125m
★ 2.5mm (B-1/UK 13) crochet hook
★ Toy stuffing
★ Tapestry needle

BODY

Work in spiral rounds. This means the rounds are not finished with a sl st, nor do you work a turning ch at the beg of a new round.

Round 1: using Black yarn, work 3 sc (UK dc) into a magic ring (3 sts).

Round 2: inc 1 st three times (6 sts).

Round 3: 1 sc (UK dc) into each st of previous round (6 sts).

Round 4: *1 sc (UK dc), inc 1 st*, rep from * to * twice more (9 sts).

Round 5: 1 sc (UK dc) into each st of previous round (9 sts).

Round 6: *2 sc (UK dc), inc 1 st*, rep from * to * twice more (12 sts).

Round 7: 1 sc (UK dc) into each st of previous round (12 sts).

Change to Yellow yarn.

Round 8: inc 1 st twelve times (24 st).

Round 9: *3 sc (UK dc), inc 1 st*, rep from * to * five more times (30 sts).

Round 10: 1 sc (UK dc) into each st of previous round (30 sts).

Round 11: *4 sc (UK dc), inc 1 st*, rep from * to * five more times (36 sts).

Round 12: 1 sc (UK dc) into each st of previous round (36 sts).

Round 13: *5 sc (UK dc), inc 1 st*, rep from * to * five more times (42 sts).

Round 14: 1 sc (UK dc) into each st of previous round (42 sts).

Round 15: *6 sc (UK dc), inc 1 st*, rep from * to * five more times (48 sts).

Change to Black yarn.

Round 16: 1 sc (UK dc) into each st of previous round (48 st).

Round 17: *7 sc (UK dc), inc 1 st*, rep from * to * five more times (54 sts).

Rounds 18 and 19: 1 sc (UK dc) into each st of previous round (54 sts).

Round 20: *8 sc (UK dc), inc 1 st*, rep from * to * five more times (60 sts).

Rounds 21–23: 1 sc (UK dc) into each st of previous round (60 sts).

Change to Yellow yarn.

Rounds 24–31: 1 sc (UK dc) into each st of previous round (60 sts).

Change to Black yarn.

Rounds 32–34: 1 sc (UK dc) into each st of previous round (60 sts).

Round 35: *8 sc (UK dc), dec 1 st*, rep from * to * five more times (54 sts).

Round 36: 1 sc (UK dc) into each st of previous round (54 sts).

Round 37: *7 sc (UK dc), dec 1 st*, rep from * to * five more times (48 sts).

Round 38: 1 sc (UK dc) into each st of previous round (48 sts).

Round 39: *6 sc (UK dc), dec 1 st*, rep from * to * five more times (42 sts).

Change to Yellow yarn.

Round 40: *5 sc (UK dc), dec 1 st*, rep from * to * five more times (36 sts).

Round 41: *4 sc (UK dc), dec 1 st*, rep from * to * five more times (30 sts).

Rounds 42 and 43: 1 sc (UK dc) into each st of previous round (30 sts).

Change to Black yarn. Stuff the body.

Round 44: *4 sc (UK dc), inc 1 st*, rep from * to * five more times (36 sts).

Round 45: *5 sc (UK dc), inc 1 st*, rep from * to * five more times (42 sts).

Rounds 46–56: 1 sc (UK dc) into each st of previous round (42 sts).

Round 57: *5 sc (UK dc), dec 1 st*, rep from * to * five more times (36 sts).

Round 58: *4 sc (UK dc), dec 1 st*, rep from * to * five more times (30 sts).

Round 59: *3 sc (UK dc), dec 1 st*, rep from * to * five more times (24 sts).

Stuff the head.

Round 60: *2 sc (UK dc), dec 1 st*, rep from * to * five more times (18 sts).

Round 61: *1 sc (UK dc), dec 1 st*, rep from * to * five more times (12 sts).

Round 62: dec 1 st six times (6 sts).

Round 63: *skip 1 st, 1 sl st*, rep from * to * twice more (3 sts).

Secure the yarn and fasten off.

ANTENNAE (MAKE 2)

Work in spiral rounds. This means the rounds are not finished with a sl st, nor do you work a turning ch at the beg of a new round.

Round 1: using Black yarn, work 6 sc (UK dc) into a magic ring (6 sts).

Round 2: inc 1 st six times (12 sts).

Rounds 3–5: 1 sc (UK dc) into each st of previous round (12 sts).

Round 6: dec 1 st six times (6 sts).

Rounds 7–14: 1 sc (UK dc) into each st of previous round (6 sts).

Secure the yarn and fasten off. Stuff the antennae.

WINGS (MAKE 2)

Work in rounds. At the end of each round, work 1 sl st into first st in round, 1 ch and turn.

Round 1: using White yarn, work 6 sc (UK dc) into a magic ring (6 sts).

Round 2: inc 1 st six times (12 sts).

Round 3: 1 sc (UK dc) into each st of previous round (12 sts).

Round 4: *1 sc (UK dc), inc 1 st*, rep from * to * five more times (18 sts).

Rounds 5–15: 1 sc (UK dc) into each st of previous round (18 sts).

Round 16: *4 sc (UK dc), dec 1 st*, rep from * to * twice more (15 sts).

Round 17: *3 sc (UK dc), dec 1 st*, rep from * to * twice more (12 sts).

Round 18: *2 sc (UK dc), dec 1 st*, rep from * to * twice more (9 sts).

Round 19: *1 sc (UK dc), dec 1 st*, rep from * to * twice more (6 sts).

Secure the yarn and fasten off. Do not stuff the wing.

EYES (MAKE 2)

Work in rounds. At the end of each round, work 1 sl st into first st in round, 1 ch and turn.

Round 1: using Black yarn, work 6 sc (UK dc) into a magic ring (6 sts).

Change to Yellow yarn.

Round 2: work into the back bar of the stitch only: inc 1 st six times (12 sts).

Secure yarn and fasten off.

LEGS (MAKE 6)

Work in spiral rounds. This means the rounds are not finished with a sl st, nor do you work a turning ch at the beg of a new round.

Round 1: using Black yarn, work 3 sc (UK dc) into a magic ring (3 sts).

Round 2: inc 1 st three times (6 sts).

Rounds 3–7: 1 sc (UK dc) into each st of previous round (6 sts).

Secure yarn and fasten off. Loosely stuff the leg.

FINISHING OFF

Sew the antennae to round 60 of the body using whip stitch. Backstitch round 2 of the eyes to the front of the body at rounds 53–56. With White yarn, embroider two French knots onto each eye. Sew the wings to the back of the body at rounds 35–43. Using Pink yarn, sew a few lines below the eyes for the cheeks and embroider a French knot between them for the mouth. Sew the legs in pairs to the front of the body.

Hettie
THE GIRAFFE

Hettie has caught a terrible cold. She has been sneezing all day. After her last big sneeze, her spots literally jumped off her body, and now adorn her scarf. She is still a beautiful giraffe, even without her spots.

HEIGHT

★ Approx. 19in (48cm)

MATERIALS

★ Lana Grossa Cool Wool Big (100% merino wool); 1 ball each of Yellow 691 and Brown 644, and scraps of Black 627 and White 601; 50g/131yd/120m
★ Austermann Merino 160 (100% merino wool); scraps of Lollipop 256; 50g/174yd/160m
★ 2.5mm (B-1/UK 13) crochet hook
★ Toy stuffing
★ Tapestry needle

HEAD, NECK AND BODY

Work in spiral rounds. This means the rounds are not finished with a sl st, nor do you work a turning ch at the beg of a new round.

Round 1: using Yellow yarn, work 6 sc (UK dc) into a magic ring (6 sts).

Round 2: inc 1 st six times (12 sts).

Round 3: *1 sc (UK dc), inc 1 st*, rep from * to * five more times (18 sts).

Round 4: *2 sc (UK dc), inc 1 st*, rep from * to * five more times (24 sts).

Round 5: 1 sc (UK dc), inc 1 st, *3 sc (UK dc), inc 1 st*, rep from * to * four more times, 2 sc (UK dc) (30 sts).

Round 6: *4 sc (UK dc), inc 1 st*, rep from * to * five more times (36 sts).

Round 7: 2 sc (UK dc), inc 1 st, *5 sc (UK dc), inc 1 st*, rep from * to * four more times, 3 sc (UK dc) (42 sts).

Round 8: *6 sc (UK dc), inc 1 st*, rep from * to * five more times (48 sts).

Round 9: 3 sc (UK dc), inc 1 st, *7 sc (UK dc), inc 1 st*, rep from * to * four more times, 4 sc (UK dc) (54 sts).

Round 10: *8 sc (UK dc), inc 1 st*, rep from * to * five more times (60 sts).

Rounds 11–17: 1 sc (UK dc) into each st of previous round (60 sts).

Round 18: *8 sc (UK dc), dec 1 st*, rep from * to * five more times (54 sts).

Round 19: 3 sc (UK dc), dec 1 st, *7 sc (UK dc), dec 1 st*, rep from * to * four more times, 4 sc (UK dc) (48 sts).

Round 20: 1 sc (UK dc) in each st of previous round (48 sts).

Round 21: *6 sc (UK dc), dec 1 st*, rep from * to * five more times (42 sts).

Round 22: *5 sc (UK dc), dec 1 st*, rep from * to * five more times (36 sts).

Round 23: *4 sc (UK dc), dec 1 st*, rep from * to * five more times (30 sts).

Stuff the head and continue as follows:

Rounds 24–44: 1 sc (UK dc) into each st of previous round (30 sts).

Round 45: 13 sc (UK dc), inc 1 st, 1 sc (UK dc), inc 1 st, 14 sc (UK dc) (32 sts).

Round 46: 9 sc (UK dc), inc 1 st, 10 sc (UK dc), inc 1 st, 11 sc (UK dc) (34 sts).

Round 47: 7 sc (UK dc), inc 1 st, 16 sc (UK dc), inc 1 st, 9 sc (UK dc) (36 sts).

Round 48: *5 sc (UK dc), inc 1 st*, rep from * to * five more times (42 sts).

Round 49: 1 sc (UK dc) into each st of previous round (42 sts).

Round 50: *6 sc (UK dc), inc 1 st*, rep from * to * five more times (48 sts).

Round 51: 12 sc (UK dc), inc 1 st, 2 sc (UK dc), inc 1 st, 4 sc (UK dc), inc 1 st twice, 4 sc (UK dc), inc 1 st, 2 sc (UK dc), inc 1 st, 18 sc (UK dc) (54 sts).

Round 52: *8 sc (UK dc), inc 1 st*, rep from * to * five more times (60 sts).

Round 53: 19 sc (UK dc), inc 1 st, 9 sc (UK dc), inc 1 st, 9 sc (UK dc), inc 1 st, 20 sc (UK dc) (63 sts).

Round 54: 1 sc (UK dc) into each st of previous round (63 sts).

Round 55: 20 sc (UK dc), inc 1 st, 10 sc (UK dc), inc 1 st, 10 sc (UK dc), inc 1 st, 20 sc (UK dc) (66 sts).

Round 56: 27 sc (UK dc), inc 1 st, 11 sc (UK dc), inc 1 st, 11 sc (UK dc), inc 1 st, 14 sc (UK dc) (69 sts).

Round 57: 21 sc (UK dc), inc 1 st, 12 sc (UK dc), inc 1 st, 12 sc (UK dc), inc 1 st, 21 sc (UK dc) (72 sts).

Round 58: 29 sc (UK dc), inc 1 st, 13 sc (UK dc), inc 1 st, 13 sc (UK dc), inc 1 st, 14 sc (UK dc) (75 sts).

Rounds 59–69: 1 sc (UK dc) into each st of previous round (75 sts).

Stuff the neck and body.

Round 70: 5 sc (UK dc), dec 1 st, 66 sc (UK dc), dec 1 st (73 sts).

Round 71: 10 sc (UK dc), dec 1 st, 54 sc (UK dc), dec 1 st, 5 sc (UK dc) (71 sts).

Round 72: 7 sc (UK dc), dec 1 st, 58 sc (UK dc), dec 1 st, 2 sc (UK dc) (69 sts).

Round 73: 1 sc (UK dc) into each st of previous round (69 sts).

Round 74: 10 sc (UK dc), dec 1 st, 50 sc (UK dc), dec 1 st, 5 sc (UK dc) (67 sts).

Round 75: 1 sc (UK dc), dec 1 st, 64 sc (UK dc) (66 sts).

Round 76: *9 sc (UK dc), dec 1 st*, rep from * to * five more times (60 sts).

Round 77: 3 sc (UK dc), dec 1 st, *8 sc (UK dc), dec 1 st*, rep from * to * four more times (54 sts).

Round 78: *7 sc (UK dc), dec 1 st*, rep from * to * five more times (48 sts).

Round 79: 2 sc (UK dc), dec 1 st, *6 sc (UK dc), dec 1 st*, rep from * to * four more times, 4 sc (UK dc) (42 sts).

Round 80: *5 sc (UK dc), dec 1 st*, rep from * to * five more times (36 sts).

Round 81: *4 sc (UK dc), dec 1 st*, rep from * to * five more times (30 sts).

Add more stuffing to the body.

Round 82: *3 sc (UK dc), dec 1 st*, rep from * to * five more times (24 sts).

Round 83: *2 sc (UK dc), dec 1 st*, rep from * to * five more times (18 sts).

Round 84: *1 sc (UK dc), dec 1 st*, rep from * to * five more times (12 sts).

Round 85: dec 1 st six times (6 sts).

Round 86: *skip 1 st, 1 sl st*, rep from * to * twice more (3 sts).

Secure the yarn and fasten off.

MUZZLE

Work in spiral rounds. This means the rounds are not finished with a sl st, nor do you work a turning ch at the beg of a new round.

Round 1: using Brown yarn, work 7 ch, 1 sc (UK dc) into second ch from hook, 1 sc (UK dc) into each of next 4 ch, 4 sc (UK dc) into last ch. Continue working on the other side of the length of ch: 4 sc (UK dc), 3 sc (UK dc) into ch with first st in (16 sts).

Round 2: 1 sc (UK dc) into each st of previous round (16 sts).

Round 3: inc 1 st, 4 sc (UK dc), inc 1 st, 10 sc (UK dc) (18 sts).

Round 4: inc 1 st, 6 sc (UK dc), inc 1 st twice, 8 sc (UK dc), inc 1 st (22 sts).

Round 5: 1 sc (UK dc) into each st of previous round (22 sts).

Round 6: 1 sc (UK dc), inc 1 st, 6 sc (UK dc), inc 1 st, 13 sc (UK dc) (24 sts).

Round 7: 3 sc (UK dc), inc 1 st, 6 sc (UK dc), inc 1 st, 13 sc (UK dc) (26 sts).

Round 8: 4 sc (UK dc), inc 1 st, 7 sc (UK dc), inc 1 st, 13 sc (UK dc) (28 sts). Change to Yellow yarn.

Round 9: inc 1 st, 3 sc (UK dc), inc 1 st, 4 sc (UK dc), inc 1 st, 4 sc (UK dc), inc 1 st, 3 sc (UK dc), inc 1 st, 4 sc (UK dc), inc 1 st, 4 sc (UK dc) (34 sts).

Round 10: 5 sc (UK dc), inc 1 st, 3 sc (UK dc), inc 1 st, 4 sc (UK dc), inc 1 st, 3 sc (UK dc), inc 1 st, 15 sc (UK dc) (38 sts).

Round 11: 1 sc (UK dc) into each st of previous round (38 sts).

Round 12: *5 sc (UK dc), inc 1 st*, rep from * to * four more times, 7 sc (UK dc), inc 1 st (44 sts).

Secure yarn and fasten off. Stuff the muzzle.

EARS (MAKE 2)

Work in spiral rounds. This means the rounds are not finished with a sl st, nor do you work a turning ch at the beg of a new round.

Round 1: using Yellow yarn, work 3 sc (UK dc) into a magic ring (3 sts).

Round 2: 1 sc (UK dc) into each st of previous round (3 sts).

Round 3: inc 1 st three times (6 sts).

Round 4: 1 sc (UK dc) into each st of previous round (6 sts).

Round 5: *1 sc (UK dc), inc 1 st*, rep from * to * twice more (9 sts).

Round 6: 1 sc (UK dc) into each st of previous round (9 sts).

Round 7: *2 sc (UK dc), inc 1 st*, rep from * to * twice more (12 sts).

Round 8: 1 sc (UK dc) into each st of previous round (12 sts).

Round 9: *3 sc (UK dc), inc 1 st*, rep from * to * twice more (15 sts).

Round 10: *4 sc (UK dc), inc 1 st*, rep from * to * twice more (18 sts).

Round 11: *5 sc (UK dc), inc 1 st*, rep from * to * twice more (21 sts).

Round 12: 1 sc (UK dc) into each st of previous round (21 sts).

Round 13: *5 sc (UK dc), dec 1 st*, rep from * to * twice more (18 sts).

Round 14: *4 sc (UK dc), dec 1 st*, rep from * to * twice more (15 sts).

Secure yarn and fasten off.

HORNS (MAKE 2)

Work in rounds. At the end of each round, work 1 sl st into first st in round, 1 ch and turn.

Round 1: using Brown yarn, work 6 sc (UK dc) into a magic ring (6 sts).

Round 2: inc 1 st six times (12 sts).

Rounds 3 and 4: 1 sc (UK dc) into each st of previous round (12 sts).

Round 5: dec 1 st six times (6 sts). Change to Yellow yarn.

Round 6: work into the back bar of the stitch only: 1 sc (UK dc) into each st of previous round (6 sts).

Round 7: 1 sc (UK dc) into each st of previous round (6 sts).

Round 8: *1 sc (UK dc), inc 1 st*, rep from * to * twice more (9 sts).

Round 9: *2 sc (UK dc), inc 1 st*, rep from * to * twice more (12 sts).

Secure yarn and fasten off. Loosely stuff the horn.

FRONT LEGS (MAKE 2)

Work in rounds. At the end of each round, work 1 sl st into first st in round, 1 ch and turn.

Round 1: using Brown yarn, work 6 sc (UK dc) into a magic ring (6 sts).

Round 2: inc 1 st six times (12 sts).

Round 3: *1 sc (UK dc), inc 1 st*, rep from * to * five more times (18 sts).

Round 4: *2 sc (UK dc), inc 1 st*, rep from * to * five more times (24 sts).

Round 5: 1 raised sc (UK dc) around the back of each st of previous round (24 sts).

Round 6: 1 sc (UK dc) into each st of previous round (24 sts).

Round 7: 9 sc (UK dc), dec 1 st, 1 sc (UK dc), dec 1 st, 1 sc (UK dc), dec 1 st, 7 sc (UK dc) (21 sts).

Round 8: 8 sc (UK dc), dec 1 st three times, 7 sc (UK dc) (18 sts).

Rounds 9 and 10: 1 sc (UK dc) into each st of previous round (18 sts). Change to Yellow yarn.

Rounds 11–23: 1 sc (UK dc) into each st of previous round (18 sts).

Round 24: dec 1 st, 16 sc (UK dc) (17 sts).

Rounds 25–30: 1 sc (UK dc) into each st of previous round (17 sts).

Round 31: 3 sc (UK dc), dec 1 st, 12 sc (UK dc) (16 sts).

Rounds 32–36: 1 sc (UK dc) into each st of previous round (16 sts).

Round 37: dec 1 st, 14 sc (UK dc) (15 sts).

Rounds 38 and 39: 1 sc (UK dc) into each st of previous round (15 sts).

Secure yarn and fasten off. Stuff the front leg.

BACK LEGS (MAKE 2)

Start working in rounds. At the end of each round, work 1 sl st into first st in round, 1 ch and turn.

Round 1: using Brown yarn, work 6 sc (UK dc) into a magic ring (6 sts).

Round 2: inc 1 st six times (12 st).

Round 3: *1 sc (UK dc), inc 1 st*, rep from * to * five more times (18 sts).

Round 4: *2 sc (UK dc), inc 1 st*, rep from * to * five more times (24 sts).

Round 5: 1 sc (UK dc), inc 1 st, *3 sc (UK dc), inc 1 st*, rep from * to * four more times, 2 sc (UK dc) (30 sts).

Round 6: *4 sc (UK dc), inc 1 st*, rep from * to * five more times (36 sts).

Round 7: 1 raised sc (UK dc) around the back of each st of previous round (36 sts).

Rounds 8 and 9: 1 sc (UK dc) into each st of previous round (36 sts).

Round 10: 10 sc (UK dc), dec 1 st eight times, 10 sc (UK dc) (28 sts).

Rounds 11 and 12: 1 sc (UK dc) into each st of previous round (28 sts).

Round 13: 10 sc (UK dc), dec 1 st four times, 10 sc (UK dc) (24 sts).

Round 14: 1 sc (UK dc) into each st of previous round (24 sts).

Change to Yellow yarn. Continue working in spiral rounds (do not sl st or turn at the end of each round).

Round 15: 10 sc (UK dc), dec 1 st, 1 sc (UK dc), dec 1 st, 9 sc (UK dc) (22 sts).

Round 16: 1 sc (UK dc), dec 1 st, 5 sc (UK dc), dec 1 st, 3 sc (UK dc), dec 1 st, 5 sc (UK dc), dec 1 st (18 sts).

Rounds 17 and 18: 1 sc (UK dc) into each st of previous round (18 sts).

Round 19: 2 sc (UK dc), dec 1 st, 4 sc (UK dc), dec 1 st, 4 sc (UK dc), dec 1 st, 2 sc (UK dc) (15 sts).

Rounds 20-26: 1 sc (UK dc) into each st of previous round (15 sts).

Round 27: 2 sc (UK dc), dec 1 st, 6 sc (UK dc), inc 1 st, 4 sc (UK dc) (15 sts).

Rounds 28–42: 1 sc (UK dc) into each st of previous round (15 sts).

Round 43: *4 sc (UK dc), inc 1 st*, rep from * to * twice more (18 sts).

Rounds 44–47: 1 sc (UK dc) into each st of previous round (18 sts).

Secure yarn and fasten off. Stuff the back leg, stuffing the last round loosely.

LARGE SPOTS (MAKE 3)

Round 1: using Yellow yarn, work 3 ch (counts as first dc (UK tr)) and 11 dc (UK tr) into a magic ring (12 sts).

Sl st to third ch of first dc (UK tr). Secure yarn and fasten off.

SMALL SPOT (MAKE 1)

Round 1: using Yellow yarn, work 6 sc (UK dc) into a magic ring (6 sts).

Sl st into first st in round. Secure yarn and fasten off.

SCARF

Work in rounds. Start each round with 3 ch as first dc (UK tr). At the end of each round, work 1 sl st into third ch of first dc (UK tr).

Using Brown yarn, work 18 ch. Work 1 sl st into first ch to make a ring.

Round 1: 1 dc (UK tr) into each st (18 sts).

Rounds 2–43: 1 dc (UK tr) into each st of previous round (18 sts).

Secure yarn and fasten off. Sew the large and small spots to the scarf.

PINK CHEEKS

Work following st into a magic ring using Lollipop yarn:

1 sc (UK dc), 1 hdc (UK htr), 1 dc (UK tr), 1 hdc (UK htr), 2 sc (UK dc), 1 hdc (UK htr), 1 dc (UK tr), 1 hdc (UK htr), 1 sc (UK dc). Join in a round with 1 sl st into the first st. Secure yarn and fasten off.

EYES (MAKE 2)

Round 1: using Black yarn, work 6 sc (UK dc) into a magic ring (6 sts).

Join in a round with 1 sl st into the first st. Secure yarn and fasten off.

FINISHING OFF

Using whip stitch, sew the last round of the muzzle to the front of the head at rounds 7–20. Press the last round of each ear together so it curves, and sew the ears the sides of the head at rounds 7–11. Sew the last round of each horn to rounds 3–5 of the head between the ears. Sew the eyes to the sides of the head, and the pink cheeks below and slightly behind them. Using White yarn, embroider two French knots onto each eye. Sew two eyelashes beside each eye in Black yarn. Press the last round of each front leg together and sew the edge to the front of the body using whip stitch. Sew the last round of each back leg to the underside of the body. Wind the scarf around the giraffe's neck, and sew together to secure.

Nelly
THE HIPPO

It's a well-known fact that hippos are great at baking. Nelly loves spending her days kneading dough, cutting out cookies – and licking the bowl when she's finished. If you visit her you're sure to come home with a basket full of baked goodies!

HEIGHT
★ Approx. 13in (33cm)

MATERIALS
★ Lang Yarns Merino 120 (100% merino wool); 2 balls of Mint 0174 and 1 ball of Rosa 0019; 50g/131yd/120m
★ Austermann Merino 160 (100% merino wool); scraps of Black 202 and White 201; 50g/174yd/160m
★ 2.5mm (B-1/UK 13) crochet hook
★ Toy stuffing
★ Tapestry needle

MUZZLE
Work in rounds. At the end of each round, work 1 sl st into first st in round, 1 ch and turn.

Round 1: using Mint yarn, work 9 ch, 1 sc (UK dc) into second ch from hook, 1 sc (UK dc) into each of next 6 ch, 3 sc (UK dc) into last ch. Continue working on the other side of the length of ch: 6 sc (UK dc), 2 sc (UK dc) into ch with first st in (18 sts).

Round 2: inc 1 st, 6 sc (UK dc), inc 1 st three times, 6 sc (UK dc), inc 1 st twice (24 sts).

Round 3: 1 sc (UK dc), inc 1 st, 7 sc (UK dc), inc 1 st, 1 sc (UK dc), inc 1 st, 1 sc (UK dc), inc 1 st, 7 sc (UK dc), inc 1 st, 1 sc (UK dc), inc 1 st (30 sts).

Round 4: 2 sc (UK dc), inc 1 st, 8 sc (UK dc), inc 1 st, 2 sc (UK dc), inc 1 st, 2 sc (UK dc), inc 1 st, 8 sc (UK dc), inc 1 st, 2 sc (UK dc), inc 1 st (36 sts).

Round 5: 3 sc (UK dc), inc 1 st, 9 sc (UK dc), inc 1 st, 3 sc (UK dc), inc 1 st, 3 sc (UK dc), inc 1 st, 9 sc (UK dc), inc 1 st, 3 sc (UK dc), inc 1 st (42 sts).

Round 6: 4 sc (UK dc), inc 1 st, 10 sc (UK dc), inc 1 st, 4 sc (UK dc), inc 1 st, 4 sc (UK dc), inc 1 st, 10 sc (UK dc), inc 1 st, 4 sc (UK dc), inc 1 st (48 sts).

Round 7: 5 sc (UK dc), inc 1 st, 11 sc (UK dc), inc 1 st, 5 sc (UK dc), inc 1 st, 5 sc (UK dc), inc 1 st, 11 sc (UK dc), inc 1 st, 5 sc (UK dc), inc 1 st (54 sts).

Round 8: 6 sc (UK dc), inc 1 st, 12 sc (UK dc), inc 1 st, 6 sc (UK dc), inc 1 st, 6 sc (UK dc), inc 1 st, 12 sc (UK dc), inc 1 st, 6 sc (UK dc), inc 1 st (60 sts).

Round 9: 7 sc (UK dc), inc 1 st, 13 sc (UK dc), inc 1 st, 7 sc (UK dc), inc 1 st, 7 sc (UK dc), inc 1 st, 13 sc (UK dc), inc 1 st, 7 sc (UK dc), inc 1 st (66 sts).

Round 10: 8 sc (UK dc), inc 1 st, 14 sc (UK dc), inc 1 st, 8 sc (UK dc), inc 1 st, 8 sc (UK dc), inc 1 st, 14 sc (UK dc), inc 1 st, 8 sc (UK dc), inc 1 st (72 sts).

Round 11: 9 sc (UK dc), inc 1 st, 15 sc (UK dc), inc 1 st, 9 sc (UK dc), inc 1 st, 9 sc (UK dc), inc 1 st, 15 sc (UK dc), inc 1 st, 9 sc (UK dc), inc 1 st (78 sts).

Round 12: 10 sc (UK dc), inc 1 st, 16 sc (UK dc), inc 1 st, 10 sc (UK dc), inc 1 st, 10 sc (UK dc), inc 1 st, 16 sc (UK dc), inc 1 st, 10 sc (UK dc), inc 1 st (84 sts).

Rounds 13–38: 1 sc (UK dc) into each st of previous round (84 sts).

Round 39: *12 sc (UK dc), dec 1 st*, rep from * to * five more times (78 sts).

Round 40: *11 sc (UK dc), dec 1 st*, rep from * to * five more times (72 sts).

Round 41: *10 sc (UK dc), dec 1 st*, rep from * to * five more times (66 sts).

Round 42: *9 sc (UK dc), dec 1 st*, rep from * to * five more times (60 sts). Stuff the muzzle.

Round 43: *8 sc (UK dc), dec 1 st*, rep from * to * five more times (54 sts).

Round 44: *7 sc (UK dc), dec 1 st*, rep from * to * five more times (48 sts).

Round 45: *6 sc (UK dc), dec 1 st*, rep from * to * five more times (42 sts).

Round 46: *5 sc (UK dc), dec 1 st*, rep from * to * five more times (36 sts).

Round 47: *4 sc (UK dc), dec 1 st*, rep from * to * five more times (30 sts).

Round 48: *3 sc (UK dc), dec 1 st*, rep from * to * five more times (24 sts).

Round 49: *2 sc (UK dc), dec 1 st*, rep from * to * five more times (18 sts).

Round 50: *1 sc (UK dc), dec 1 st*, rep from * to * five more times (12 sts).

Round 51: dec 1 st six times (6 sts).

Round 52: *skip 1 st, 1 sl st*, rep from * to * twice more (3 sts). Secure the yarn and fasten off.

TOP OF HEAD
Work in rounds. At the end of each round, work 1 sl st into first st in round, 1 ch and turn.

Round 1: using Mint yarn, work 17 ch, 1 sc (UK dc) into second ch from hook, 1 sc (UK dc) into each of next 14 ch, 3 sc (UK dc) into last ch. Continue working on the other side of the length of ch: 14 sc (UK dc), 2 sc (UK dc) into ch with first st in (34 sts).

Round 2: inc 1 st, 14 sc (UK dc), inc 1 st three times, 14 sc (UK dc), inc 1 st twice (40 sts).

Round 3: 1 sc (UK dc), inc 1 st, 15 sc (UK dc), inc 1 st, 1 sc (UK dc), inc 1 st, 1 sc (UK dc), inc 1 st, 15 sc (UK dc), inc 1 st, 1 sc (UK dc), inc 1 st (46 sts).

Round 4: 2 sc (UK dc), inc 1 st, 16 sc (UK dc), inc 1 st, 2 sc (UK dc), inc 1 st, 2 sc (UK dc), inc 1 st, 16 sc (UK dc), inc 1 st, 2 sc (UK dc), inc 1 st (52 sts).

Round 5: 3 sc (UK dc), inc 1 st, 17 sc (UK dc), inc 1 st, 3 sc (UK dc), inc 1 st, 3 sc (UK dc), inc 1 st, 17 sc (UK dc), inc 1 st, 3 sc (UK dc), inc 1 st (58 sts).

Round 6: 4 sc (UK dc), inc 1 st, 18 sc (UK dc), inc 1 st, 4 sc (UK dc), inc 1 st, 4 sc (UK dc), inc 1 st, 18 sc (UK dc), inc 1 st, 4 sc (UK dc), inc 1 st (64 sts).

Rounds 7-15: 1 sc (UK dc) into each st of previous round (64 sts).

Secure yarn and fasten off.

BODY

Work in rounds. At the end of each round, work 1 sl st into first st in round, 1 ch and turn.

Round 1: using Mint yarn, work 6 sc (UK dc) into a magic ring (6 sts).

Round 2: inc 1 st six times (12 sts).

Round 3: *1 sc (UK dc), inc 1 st*, rep from * to * five more times (18 sts).

Round 4: *2 sc (UK dc), inc 1 st*, rep from * to * five more times (24 sts).

Round 5: *3 sc (UK dc), inc 1 st*, rep from * to * five more times (30 sts).

Round 6: *4 sc (UK dc), inc 1 st*, rep from * to * five more times (36 sts).

Round 7: *5 sc (UK dc), inc 1 st*, rep from * to * five more times (42 sts).

Round 8: *6 sc (UK dc), inc 1 st*, rep from * to * five more times (48 sts).

Round 9: *7 sc (UK dc), inc 1 st*, rep from * to * five more times (54 sts).

Round 10: *8 sc (UK dc), inc 1 st*, rep from * to * five more times (60 sts).

Round 11: *9 sc (UK dc), inc 1 st*, rep from * to * five more times (66 sts).

Round 12: *10 sc (UK dc), inc 1 st*, rep from * to * five more times (72 sts).

Rounds 13–16: 1 sc (UK dc) into each st of previous round (72 sts).

Round 17: *11 sc (UK dc), inc 1 st*, rep from * to * five more times (78 sts).

Rounds 18–32: 1 sc (UK dc) into each st of previous round (78 sts).

Round 33: *11 sc (UK dc), dec 1 st*, rep from * to * five more times (72 sts).

Round 34: *10 sc (UK dc), dec 1 st*, rep from * to * five more times (66 sts).

Round 35: *9 sc (UK dc), dec 1 st*, rep from * to * five more times (60 sts).

Round 36: *8 sc (UK dc), dec 1 st*, rep from * to * five more times (54 sts).

Round 37: *7 sc (UK dc), dec 1 st*, rep from * to * five more times (48 sts).

Round 38: *6 sc (UK dc), dec 1 st*, rep from * to * five more times (42 sts).

Round 39: *5 sc (UK dc), dec 1 st*, rep from * to * five more times (36 sts).

Secure yarn and fasten off. Stuff the body.

LEGS (MAKE 2)

Work in rounds. At the end of each round, work 1 sl st into first st in round, 1 ch and turn.

Round 1: using Rosa yarn, work 6 sc (UK dc) into a magic ring (6 sts).

Round 2: inc 1 st six times (12 st).

Change to Mint yarn.

Rounds 3–12: 1 sc (UK dc) into each st of previous round (12 sts).

Secure yarn and fasten off. Stuff the leg.

ARMS (MAKE 2)

Crochet the arms as the legs, working two additional rounds of round 12.

EARS (MAKE 2 ROSA, 2 MINT)

Work in rounds. At the end of each round, work 1 sl st into first st in round, 1 ch and turn.

Round 1: work 5 ch, 1 sc (UK dc) into second ch from hook, 1 sc (UK dc) into each of next 2 ch, 3 sc (UK dc) into last ch. Continue working on the other side of the length of ch: 2 sc (UK dc), 2 sc (UK dc) into ch with first st in (10 sts).

Round 2: 4 sc (UK dc), inc 1 st, 4 sc (UK dc), inc 1 st (12 sts).

Secure yarn and fasten off.

Place one of each colour ear together; hold so that you are looking at the ear in Mint yarn. Using Mint yarn, work 1 round sc (UK dc) around to join.

EYES (MAKE 2)

Round 1: using Black yarn, work 6 sc (UK dc) into a magic ring (6 sts).

Join in a round with 1 sl st into the first st in the round. Secure the yarn and fasten off.

NOSTRILS (MAKE 2)

Work in rounds. At the end of each round, work 1 sl st into first st in round, 1 ch and turn.

Round 1: using Rosa yarn, work 6 sc (UK dc) into a magic ring (6 sts).

Round 2: inc 1 st six times (12 sts).

Secure the yarn and fasten off.

FINISHING OFF

Sew the last round of the top of the head to the muzzle, working from the middle to the edge. When finished the first round of the muzzle should be facing forward and the first round of the top of the muzzle facing up. Sew the last round of the body to the underside of the muzzle using mattress stitch. Sew the last round of the arms to the sides of the body using whip stitch. Sew the last round of the legs to the underside of the body using whip stitch. Sew an ear to each side of the top of the head. Position the eyes 10 sts apart above the muzzle, and sew to the top of the head. Using White yarn, embroider two French knots onto each eye, and sew two eyelashes beside each eye in Black yarn. Sew a nostril to each side of the muzzle.

Agatha
THE ZEBRA

Agatha is a famous gymnast. Her house is absolutely bursting with medals and trophies she's won. Her favourite thing is doing the splits – and she spontaneously does them all over the place.

HEIGHT
★ Approx. 12½in (32cm)

MATERIAL
★ Lang Yarns Merino 70 Dégradé (98% merino wool, 2% polyester); 1 ball of Fuchsia/Grey/Brown 0066; 100g/153yd/140m
★ Lang Yarns Merino 70 (98% merino wool, 2% polyester); 2 balls of Off-white 0094; 100g/76yd/70m
★ Austermann Merino 160 (100% merino wool); scraps of Black 202 and White 201; 50g/174yd/160m
★ 4mm (G-6/UK 8) and 2.5mm (B-1/UK 13) crochet hooks
★ Toy stuffing
★ Tapestry needle

HEAD
Work in rounds. At the end of each round, work 1 sl st into first st in round, 1 ch and turn.

Round 1: using 4mm (G-6/UK 8) hook and Fuchsia/Grey/Brown yarn, work 6 sc (UK dc) into a magic ring (6 sts).

Round 2: inc 1 st six times (12 sts).

Round 3: *1 sc (UK dc), inc 1 st*, rep from * to * five more times (18 sts).

Round 4: *2 sc (UK dc), inc 1 st*, rep from * to * five more times (24 sts).

Round 5: *3 sc (UK dc), inc 1 st*, rep from * to * five more times (30 sts).

Round 6: *4 sc (UK dc), inc 1 st*, rep from * to * five more times (36 sts).

Rounds 7–14: 1 sc (UK dc) into each st of previous round (36 sts).

Round 15: 15 sc (UK dc), [inc 1 st, 2 sc (UK dc), inc 1 st, 2 sc (UK dc), inc 1 st], (the st in square brackets will be on the top of the finished zebra's head), 14 sc (UK dc) (39 sts). Change to Off-white yarn.
From this point, change to Fuchsia/Grey/Brown or Off-white yarn every 2 rounds.

Rounds 16–29: 1 sc (UK dc) into each st of previous round (39 sts).

Round 30: *11 sc (UK dc), dec 1 st*, rep from * to * twice more (36 sts).

Round 31: *4 sc (UK dc), dec 1 st*, rep from * to * five more times (30 sts).
Stuff the head.
Change to Off-white yarn. Do not change back to Fuchsia/Grey/Brown yarn, again.

Round 32: *3 sc (UK dc), dec 1 st*, rep from * to * five more times (24 sts).

Round 33: *2 sc (UK dc), dec 1 st*, rep from * to * five more times (18 sts).

Round 34: *1 sc (UK dc), dec 1 st*, rep from * to * five more times (12 sts).

Round 35: dec 1 st six times (6 sts).

Round 36: *skip 1 st, 1 sl st*, rep from * to * twice more (3 sts).
Secure the yarn and fasten off.

BODY
Work in rounds. At the end of each round, work 1 sl st into first st in round, 1 ch and turn. Change to Off-white or Fuchsia/Grey/Brown yarn every 2 rounds.

Round 1: using 4mm (G-6/UK 8) hook and Fuchsia/Grey/Brown yarn, work 6 sc (UK dc) into a magic ring (6 sts).

Round 2: inc 1 st six times (12 sts).

Round 3: *1 sc (UK dc), inc 1 st*, rep from * to * five more times (18 sts).

Round 4: *2 sc (UK dc), inc 1 st*, rep from * to * five more times (24 sts).

Round 5: *3 sc (UK dc), inc 1 st*, rep from * to * five more times (30 sts).

Round 6: *4 sc (UK dc), inc 1 st*, rep from * to * five more times (36 sts).

Rounds 7–24: 1 sc (UK dc) into each st of previous round (36 sts).

Round 25: *2 sc (UK dc), dec 1 st*, rep from * to * five more times, 12 sc (UK dc) (30 sts).

Round 26: *1 sc (UK dc), dec 1 st*, rep from * to * five more times, 12 sc (UK dc) (24 sts).

Round 27: dec 1 st six times, 12 sc (UK dc) (18 sts).

Stuff the body.

Round 28: *1 sc (UK dc), dec 1 st*, rep from * to * five more times (12 sts).

Round 29: dec 1 st six times (6 sts).

Round 30: *skip 1 st, 1 sl st *, rep from * to * twice more (3 sts).
Secure yarn and fasten off.

LEGS (MAKE 2)
Work in rounds. At the end of each round, work 1 sl st into first st in round, 1 ch and turn.

Round 1: using 4mm (G-6/UK 8) hook and Fuchsia/Grey/Brown yarn, work 6 sc (UK dc) into a magic ring (6 sts).

Round 2: inc 1 st six times (12 sts).

Round 3: *1 sc (UK dc), inc 1 st*, rep from * to * five more times (18 sts).

Round 4: *2 sc (UK dc), inc 1 st*, rep from * to * five more times (24 sts).

Rounds 5–8: 1 sc (UK dc) into each st of previous round (24 sts).
Change to Off-white yarn.

Rounds 9 and 10: 1 sc (UK dc) into each st of previous round (24 sts).
Change to Fuchsia/Grey/Brown yarn.

Rounds 11 and 12: 1 sc (UK dc) into each st of previous round (24 sts).
Change to Off-white yarn.

Rounds 13 and 14: 1 sc (UK dc) into each st of previous round (24 sts).
Change to Fuchsia/Grey/Brown yarn.

Round 15: 1 sc (UK dc) into each st of previous round (24 sts).

Round 16: *2 sc (UK dc), dec 1 st*, rep from * to * five more times (18 sts).
Change to Off-white yarn.

Round 17: 1 sc (UK dc) into each st of previous round (18 sts).

Round 18: *1 sc (UK dc), dec 1 st*, rep from * to * five more times (12 sts).
Secure the yarn and fasten off. Stuff the leg, but not quite as far as the opening.

ARMS (MAKE 2)

Work in rounds. At the end of each round, work 1 sl st into first st in round, 1 ch and turn.

Round 1: using 4mm (G-6/UK 8) hook and Fuchsia/Grey/Brown yarn, work 6 sc (UK dc) into a magic ring (6 sts).

Round 2: inc 1 st six times (12 sts).

Rounds 3–5: 1 sc (UK dc) into each st of previous round (12 sts).
Change to Off-white yarn. From here change to Fuchsia/Grey/Brown or Off-white yarn every 2 rounds.

Rounds 6–23: 1 sc (UK dc) into each st of previous round (12 sts).
Secure yarn and fasten off. Do not stuff the arms.

EARS (MAKE 2)

Work in spiral rounds. This means the rounds are not finished with a sl st, nor do you work a turning ch at the beg of a new round.

Round 1: using 4mm (G-6/UK 8) hook and Fuchsia/Grey/Brown yarn, work 3 sc (UK dc) into a magic ring (3 sts).

Round 2: inc 1 st three times (6 sts).

Round 3: *1 sc (UK dc), inc 1 st*, rep from * to * twice more (9 sts).

Round 4: *2 sc (UK dc), inc 1 st*, rep from * to * twice more (12 sts).

Rounds 5–9: 1 sc (UK dc) into each st of previous round (12 sts).

Round 10: *2 sc (UK dc), dec 1 st*, rep from * to * twice more (9 sts).

Round 11: *1 sc (UK dc), dec 1 st*, rep from * to * twice more (6 sts).

Round 12: *skip 1 st, 1 sl st*, rep from * to * twice more (3 sts).
Secure the yarn and fasten off.

TAIL

Join Fuchsia/Grey/Brown yarn to round 10 of the back of the body, and using 4mm (G-6/UK 8) hook, work 21 ch. 1 sl st into 7th ch from the hook, *6 ch, 1 sl st into 7th ch*, rep from * to * twice more. Work 1 sl st into each of the remaining 14 ch.

EYES

Round 1: Using 2.5mm (B-1/UK 13) hook and Black yarn, work 6 sc (UK dc) into a magic ring (6 sts).
Join in a round with 1 sl st into the first st in the round. Secure the yarn and fasten off.

FINISHING OFF

Sew the head to the last round of the body using mattress stitch. Sew the last round of each arm to the side of the body at round 24. To secure, sew round 4 of the arms to the zebra's tummy with a few stitches. Press the last round of each leg together, and sew to the side of the body at round 7. Sew the ears to round 27 of the head. Attach the eyes to rounds 17 and 18 of the head. Using White yarn, embroider two French knots to each eye and sew two eyelashes in Black yarn beside each eye. For the mane, join Fuchsia/Grey/Brown yarn to the top of the head between the ears, and knot securely. Cut to the desired length. Repeat several times until you have the desired amount of hair.

Louis
THE LION

Louis is the most relaxed King that the animal world has ever seen. Always cheerful and happy, he prefers throwing parties instead of troubling himself with the serious things in life.

HEIGHT
★ Approx. 9in (23cm)

MATERIAL
★ Lang Yarns Merino 120 (100% merino wool); 2 balls of Burnt Orange 0159, 1 ball of Yellow 0149, and small amounts of Bright Red 0160; 50g/131yd/120m
★ Austermann Merino 160 (100% merino wool); scraps of Black 202 and White 201; 50g/174yd/160m
★ 2.5mm (B-1/UK 13) crochet hook
★ Toy stuffing
★ Tapestry needle

BODY
Work in rounds. At the end of each round, work 1 sl st into first st in round, 1 ch and turn.

Round 1: using Burnt Orange yarn, work 6 sc (UK dc) into a magic ring (6 sts).

Round 2: inc 1 st six times (12 sts).

Round 3: *1 sc (UK dc), inc 1 st*, rep from * to * five more times (18 sts).

Round 4: *2 sc (UK dc), inc 1 st*, rep from * to * five more times (24 sts).

Round 5: *3 sc (UK dc), inc 1 st*, rep from * to * five more times (30 sts).

Round 6: *4 sc (UK dc), inc 1 st*, rep from * to * five more times (36 sts).

Round 7: *5 sc (UK dc), inc 1 st*, rep from * to * five more times (42 sts).

Round 8: *6 sc (UK dc), inc 1 st*, rep from * to * five more times (48 sts).

Round 9: *7 sc (UK dc), inc 1 st*, rep from * to * five more times (54 sts).

Round 10: *8 sc (UK dc), inc 1 st*, rep from * to * five more times (60 sts).

Round 11: *9 sc (UK dc), inc 1 st*, rep from * to * five more times (66 sts).

Round 12: *10 sc (UK dc), inc 1 st*, rep from * to * five more times (72 sts).

Round 13: *11 sc (UK dc), inc 1 st*, rep from * to * five more times (78 sts).

Round 14: *12 sc (UK dc), inc 1 st*, rep from * to * five more times (84 sts).

Round 15: *13 sc (UK dc), inc 1 st*, rep from * to * five more times (90 sts).

Rounds 16–55: 1 sc (UK dc) into each st of previous round (90 sts).

Round 56: *13 sc (UK dc), dec 1 st*, rep from * to * five more times (84 sts).

Round 57: *12 sc (UK dc), dec 1 st*, rep from * to * five more times (78 sts).

Round 58: *11 sc (UK dc), dec 1 st*, rep from * to * five more times (72 sts).

Round 59: *10 sc (UK dc), dec 1 st*, rep from * to * five more times (66 sts).

Round 60: *9 sc (UK dc), dec 1 st*, rep from * to * five more times (60 sts).
Stuff the body.

Round 61: *8 sc (UK dc), dec 1 st*, rep from * to * five more times (54 sts).

Round 62: *7 sc (UK dc), dec 1 st*, rep from * to * five more times (48 sts).

Round 63: *6 sc (UK dc), dec 1 st*, rep from * to * five more times (42 sts).

Round 64: *5 sc (UK dc), dec 1 st*, rep from * to * five more times (36 sts).

Round 65: *4 sc (UK dc), dec 1 st*, rep from * to * five more times (30 sts).
Stuff the remainder of the body.

Round 66: *3 sc (UK dc), dec 1 st*, rep from * to * five more times (24 sts).

Round 67: *2 sc (UK dc), dec 1 st*, rep from * to * five more times (18 sts).

Round 68: *1 sc (UK dc), dec 1 st*, rep from * to * five more times (12 sts).

Round 69: dec 1 st six times (6 sts).

Round 70: *skip 1 st, 1 sl st*, rep from * to * twice more (3 sts).
Secure the yarn and fasten off.

HEAD

Work in rows. At the end of each row, work 1 ch to turn.

Row 1: using Yellow yarn, work 25 ch, 1 sc (UK dc) into second ch from hook, 1 sc (UK dc) into the remaining ch (24 sts).

Rows 2–24: 1 sc (UK dc) into each st of previous row (24 sts).

Secure the yarn and fasten off.

Rep rows 1–24. You will have two square pieces. Place the two squares together and work 1 sc (UK dc) into each st along the edges to join together. Work 2 sc (UK dc) into each corner st. Stuff the head before closing. Do not fasten off, but continue working:

MANE

Work 1 round as follows into the back bar of the st only of the previous round and repeat until you have worked once around the head:

2 sl st, 12 ch, 1 sl st into same st as previous sl st.

Secure yarn and fasten off.

Join Bright Red yarn to the front of the first st in the edge round of the head, and work 1 round as follows:

1 sl st, 5 ch, 1 sl st into same st as previous sl st, rep from * to * to the end of the round.

Secure the yarn and fasten off.

TAIL

Work in spiral rounds. This means the rounds are not finished with a sl st, nor do you work a turning ch at the beg of a new round. Place a marker at beg of round to make it easier to find.

Round 1: using Bright Red yarn, work 6 sc (UK dc) into a magic ring (6 sts).

Rounds 2–19: 1 sc (UK dc) into each st of previous round (6 sts).

Change to Yellow yarn.

Round 20: inc 1 st six times (12 sts).

Rounds 21–23: 1 sc (UK dc) into each st of previous round (12 sts).

Round 24: *2 sc (UK dc), dec 1 st*, rep from * to * twice more (9 sts).

Round 25: 1 sc (UK dc) into each st of previous round (9 sts).

Round 26: *1 sc (UK dc), dec 1 st*, rep from * to * twice more (6 sts).

Round 27: 1 sc (UK dc) into each st of previous round (6 sts).

Round 28: *skip 1 st, 1 sl st*, rep from * to * twice more (3 sts).

Secure yarn and fasten off.

LEGS (MAKE 4)

Work in spiral rounds. This means the rounds are not finished with a sl st, nor do you work a turning ch at the beg of a new round. Place a marker at beg of round to make it easier to find.

Work three legs in Burnt Orange yarn and one striped in the col sequence Burnt Orange – Bright Red – Yellow.

Round 1: work 6 sc (UK dc) into a magic ring (6 sts).

Round 2: inc 1 st three times, 3 sc (UK dc) (9 sts).

Round 3: *1 sc (UK dc), inc 1 st*, rep from * to * twice more, 3 sc (UK dc) (12 sts).

Round 4: *2 sc (UK dc), inc 1 st*, rep from * to * twice more, 3 sc (UK dc) (15 sts).

Rounds 5-11: 1 sc (UK dc) into each st of previous round (15 sts).

Secure yarn and fasten off. Stuff the legs.

EYES (MAKE 2)

Round 1: using Black yarn, work 6 sc (UK dc) into a magic ring (6 sts).

Join in a round with 1 sl st into the first st. Secure the yarn and fasten off.

EARS (MAKE 2)

Round 1: using Bright Red yarn, work 4 ch, 1 sc (UK dc) and 1 hdc (UK htr) into second ch from hook, 4 dc (UK tr) into next ch, 1 hdc (UK htr) and 1 sl st into last ch.

Secure the yarn and fasten off.

FINISHING OFF

Sew the last round of two of the legs in Burnt Orange yarn to rounds 46–51 of the body using whip stitch. Sew the last round of one of the legs in Burnt Orange yarn and the striped leg to rounds 19–24 of the body using whip stitch. Sew the magic ring for the tail to round 59 of the body. Secure the tip of the tail to the back of the lion with a few stitches. Sew the eyes to the lion's face and, using White yarn, embroider two French knots to each eye. Using Black yarn sew two eyelashes beside each eye. Sew a few lines in Black yarn in the middle of the face, below the eyes, for the nose. For the mouth, use Black yarn and sew one vertical line and two diagonal lines, like an arrow from the nose. Sew one ear to each side of the head above the eyes. Sew the head to rounds 11–25 of the body.

Victor
THE OSTRICH

Victor is the fastest runner, and no one can keep up with him. But on the rare occasions when he loses, his favourite thing to do to cheer himself up is to go dancing. Even with his big feet he has some great moves.

Let's Go

HEIGHT
★ Approx. 15in (38cm)

MATERIALS
★ Austermann Merino 160 (100% merino wool); 2 balls of Black 202, 1 ball each of Natur 210 and Make Up 244, and scraps of Orange 205; 50g/174yd/160m
★ 2.5mm (B-1/UK 13) crochet hook
★ Toy stuffing
★ Tapestry needle

BODY
Work in rounds. At the end of each round, work 1 sl st into first st in round, 1 ch and turn.

Round 1: using Natur yarn, work 6 sc (UK dc) into a magic ring (6 sts).

Round 2: inc 1 st six times (12 sts).

Round 3: *1 sc (UK dc), inc 1 st*, rep from * to * five more times (18 sts).

Round 4: 1 sc (UK dc) into each st of previous round (18 sts).

Round 5: *2 sc (UK dc), inc 1 st*, rep from * to * five more times (24 sts).

Round 6: *3 sc (UK dc), inc 1 st*, rep from * to * five more times (30 sts).

Round 7: *4 sc (UK dc), inc 1 st*, rep from * to * five more times (36 sts).

Round 8: 1 sc (UK dc) into each st of previous round (36 sts).

Round 9: *5 sc (UK dc), inc 1 st*, rep from * to * five more times (42 sts).

Round 10: *6 sc (UK dc), inc 1 st*, rep from * to * five more times (48 sts).

Round 11: *7 sc (UK dc), inc 1 st*, rep from * to * five more times (54 sts).

Round 12: 1 sc (UK dc) into each st of previous round (54 sts).
Change to Black yarn.

Round 13: *8 sc (UK dc), inc 1 st*, rep from * to * five more times (60 sts).

Round 14: *9 sc (UK dc), inc 1 st*, rep from * to * five more times (66 sts).

Round 15: *10 sc (UK dc), inc 1 st*, rep from * to * five more times (72 sts).

Round 16: 1 sc (UK dc) into each st of previous round (72 sts).

Round 17: *11 sc (UK dc), inc 1 st*, rep from * to * five more times (78 sts).

Round 18: *12 sc (UK dc), inc 1 st*, rep from * to * five more times (84 sts).

Round 19: *13 sc (UK dc), inc 1 st*, rep from * to * five more times (90 sts).

Round 20: *14 sc (UK dc), inc 1 st*, rep from * to * five more times (96 sts).

Rounds 21–35: 1 sc (UK dc) into each st of previous round (96 sts).

Round 36: *14 sc (UK dc), dec 1 st*, rep from * to * five more times (90 sts).

Rounds 37 and 38: 1 sc (UK dc) into each st of previous round (90 sts).

Round 39: 2 sc (UK dc), dec 1 st, 4 sc (UK dc), dec 1 st, 4 sc (UK dc), dec 1 st, 60 sc (UK dc), dec 1 st, 4 sc (UK dc), dec 1 st, 4 sc (UK dc), dec 1 st (84 sts).

Rounds 40 and 41: 1 sc (UK dc) into each st of previous round (84 sts).

Round 42: dec 1 st, 3 sc (UK dc), dec 1 st, 3 sc (UK dc), dec 1 st, 59 sc (UK dc), dec 1 st, 3 sc (UK dc), dec 1 st, 3 sc (UK dc), dec 1 st, 1 sc (UK dc) (78 sts).

Round 43: 1 sc (UK dc) into each st of previous round (78 sts).

Round 44: *11 sc (UK dc), dec 1 st*, rep from * to * five more times (72 sts).

Round 45: *4 sc (UK dc), dec 1 st*, rep from * to * twice more, 36 sc (UK dc), *dec 1 st, 4 sc (UK dc)*, rep from * to * twice more (66 sts).

Round 46: 1 sc (UK dc) in each st of previous round (66 sts).

Round 47: *9 sc (UK dc), dec 1 st*, rep from * to * five more times (60 sts).

Round 48: *3 sc (UK dc), dec 1 st*, rep from * to * twice more, 30 sc (UK dc), *dec 1 st, 3 sc (UK dc)*, rep from * to * twice more (54 sts).

Round 49: 1 sc (UK dc) into each st of previous round (54 sts). Stuff the body.

Round 50: *7 sc (UK dc), dec 1 st*, rep from * to * five more times (48 sts).

Round 51: *6 sc (UK dc), dec 1 st*, rep from * to * five more times (42 sts).
Change to Natur yarn.

Round 52: work into the back bar of the stitch only: 1 sc (UK dc) into each st of previous round (42 sts).

Round 53: work into the back bar of the stitch only: *5 sc (UK dc), dec 1 st*, rep from * to * five more times (36 sts).

Round 54: work into the back bar of the stitch only: *4 sc (UK dc), dec 1 st*, rep from * to * five more times (36 sts).

Round 55: *3 sc (UK dc), dec 1 st*, rep from * to * five more times (24 sts).
Change to Make Up yarn.

Rounds 56–59: 1 sc (UK dc) into each st of previous round (24 sts).

Round 60: 1 sc (UK dc), dec 1 st, 1 sc (UK dc), dec 1 st, 8 sc (UK dc), inc 1 st, 1 sc (UK dc), inc 1 st, 7 sc (UK dc) (24 sts).

Round 61: 1 sc (UK dc) into each st of previous round (24 st).

Round 62: dec 1 st, 1 sc (UK dc), dec 1 st, 8 sc (UK dc), inc 1 st, 1 sc (UK dc), inc 1 st, 8 sc (UK dc) (24 sts).

Round 68: skip 1 st, 1 sc (UK dc), skip 1 st, 8 sc (UK dc), inc 1 st, 1 sc (UK dc), inc 1 st, 10 sc (UK dc) (24 sts).

Round 69: 1 sc (UK dc) into each st of previous round (24 sts).

Round 70: dec 1 st, 9 sc (UK dc), inc 1 st, 1 sc (UK dc), inc 1 st, 9 sc (UK dc) (24 sts).

Round 71: 1 sc (UK dc) into each st of previous round (24 sts).

Secure yarn and fasten off. Stuff the remainder of the body.

COLLAR

Join Natur yarn to the front bar of the first st of round 52 of the body, and work one round: *2 hdc (UK htr) in 1 st, 3 hdc (UK htr) in 1 st*, rep from * to * to the end of round. Secure the yarn and fasten off.

HEAD

Work in spiral rounds. This means the rounds are not finished with a sl st, nor do you work a turning ch at the beg of a new round.

Round 1: using Make Up yarn, work 6 sc (UK dc) into a magic ring (6 sts).

Round 2: inc 1 st six times (12 sts).

Round 3: *1 sc (UK dc), inc 1 st*, rep from * to * five more times (18 sts).

Round 4: *2 sc (UK dc), inc 1 st*, rep from * to * five more times (24 sts).

Round 5: *3 sc (UK dc), inc 1 st*, rep from * to * five more times (30 sts).

Round 6: *4 sc (UK dc), inc 1 st*, rep from * to * five more times (36 sts).

Round 7: *5 sc (UK dc), inc 1 st*, rep from * to * five more times (42 sts).

Rounds 8–16: 1 sc (UK dc) into each st of previous round (42 sts).

Round 17: *2 sc (UK dc), dec 1 st*, rep from * to * five more times, 18 sc (UK dc) (36 sts).

Round 18: 1 sc (UK dc) into each st of previous round (36 sts).

Round 19: *4 sc (UK dc), dec 1 st*, rep from * to * five more times (30 sts).

Round 20: 1 sc (UK dc) into each st of previous round (30 sts).

Round 21: *1 sc (UK dc), dec 1 st*, rep from * to * five more times, 12 sc (UK dc) (24 sts).

Stuff the head.

Round 22: 1 sc (UK dc) into each st of previous round (24 sts).

Round 23: *2 sc (UK dc), dec 1 st*, rep from * to * five more times (18 sts).

Round 24: *1 sc (UK dc), dec 1 st*, rep from * to * five more times (12 sts).

Round 25: dec 1 st six times (6 sts).

Round 26: *skip 1 st, 1 sl st*, rep from * to * twice more (3 sts).

Secure the yarn and fasten off.

BEAK

Work in rounds. At the end of each round, work 1 sl st into first st in round, 1 ch and turn.

Round 1: using Orange yarn, work 3 sc (UK dc) into a magic ring (3 sts).

Round 2: inc 1 st three times (6 sts).

Round 3: 1 sc (UK dc) into each st of previous round (6 sts).

Round 4: *1 sc (UK dc), inc 1 st*, rep from * to * twice more (9 sts).

Round 5: 1 sc (UK dc) into each st of previous round (9 sts).

Round 6: *2 sc (UK dc), inc 1 st*, rep from * to * twice more (12 sts).

Round 7: *3 sc (UK dc), inc 1 st*, rep from * to * twice more (15 sts).

Round 8: 3 sc (UK dc), inc 1 st twice, 10 sc (UK dc) (17 sts).

Secure the yarn and fasten off. Stuff the beak.

EYES (MAKE 2)

Round 1: using Black yarn, work 6 sc (UK dc) into a magic ring (6 sts).

Join in a round with 1 sl st into the first st. Secure the yarn and fasten off.

LEGS (MAKE 2)

Round 1: using Make Up yarn, work 6 sc (UK dc) into a magic ring in (6 sts).

Rounds 2–3: 1 sc (UK dc) in each st of the previous round (6 sts).

Round 63: 1 sc (UK dc) into each st of previous round (24 sts).

Round 64: skip 1 st, 1 sc (UK dc), skip 1 st, 10 sc (UK dc), inc 1 st, 1 sc (UK dc), inc 1 st, 8 sc (UK dc) (24 sts).

Round 65: 1 sc (UK dc) in each st of previous round (24 sts).

Round 66: skip 1 st, 1 sc (UK dc), skip 1 st, 9 sc (UK dc), inc 1 st, 1 sc (UK dc), inc 1 st, 9 sc (UK dc) (24 sts).

Round 67: 1 sc (UK dc) into each st of previous round (24 sts).

Secure the yarn and fasten off. Crochet two more toes. Do not fasten off the yarn of the third (referred to in the following as "the first toe"), but continue crocheting as follows:

Round 4: 3 sc (UK dc) in the first toe, 3 sc (UK dc) in the second toe, 6 sc (UK dc) in the last toe, 3 sc (UK dc) in the remaining st of the second toe, 3 sc (UK dc) in the remaining st of the first toe (18 sts).

Rounds 5 and 6: 1 sc (UK dc) into each st of previous round (18 sts).

Round 7: *4 sc (UK dc), dec 1 st*, rep from * to * twice more (15 sts).

Round 8: *3 sc (UK dc), dec 1 st*, rep from * to * twice more (12 sts).

Round 9: 1 sc (UK dc) into each st of previous round (12 sts).

Round 10: *2 sc (UK dc), dec 1 st*, rep from * to * twice more (9 sts).

Rounds 11–35: 1 sc (UK dc) into each st of previous round (9 sts).

Round 36: inc 1 st three times (these should be above where the three toes are lying flat in a line), 1 sc (UK dc) into each of the remaining st in the round (12 sts).

Round 37: continue working over the 3 inc in the previous round: *1 sc (UK dc), inc 1 st*, rep from * to * twice more. Work 1 sc (UK dc) into each of the remaining st in the round (15 sts).

Rounds 38–43: 1 sc (UK dc) into each st of previous round (12 sts).

Secure the yarn and fasten off. Stuff the leg.

WINGS (MAKE 2)

Work in rounds. At the end of each round, work 1 sl st into first st in round, 1 ch and turn.

Round 1: using Natur yarn, work 6 sc (UK dc) into a magic ring (6 st).

Round 2: *1 sc (UK dc), inc 1 st*, rep from * to * twice more (9 sts).

Round 3: *2 sc (UK dc), inc 1 st*, rep from * to * twice more (12 sts).

Round 4: 1 sc (UK dc) into each st of previous round (12 sts).

Round 5: *1 sc (UK dc), inc 1 st*, rep from * to * five more times (18 sts).

Round 6: 1 sc (UK dc) into each st of previous round (18 sts).

Round 7: *1 sc (UK dc), inc 1 st*, rep from * to * eight more times (27 sts).

Round 8: *2 sc (UK dc), inc 1 st*, rep from * to * five more times (36 sts).

Change to Black yarn.

Rounds 9–13: 1 sc (UK dc) into each st of previous round (36 sts).

Round 14: *5 sc (UK dc), inc 1 st*, rep from * to * five more times (42 sts).

Round 15: 1 sc (UK dc) into each st of previous round (42 sts).

Round 16: *6 sc (UK dc), inc 1 st*, rep from * to * five more times (48 sts).

Round 17: 1 sc (UK dc) into each st of previous round (48 sts).

Round 18: *7 sc (UK dc), inc 1 st*, rep from * to * five more times (54 sts).

Rounds 19–27: 1 sc (UK dc) into each st of previous round (54 sts).

Round 28: *7 sc (UK dc), dec 1 st*, rep from * to * five more times (48 sts).

Round 29: 1 sc (UK dc) into each st of previous round (48 sts).

Round 30: dec 1 st, 3 sc (UK dc), dec 1 st, 3 sc (UK dc), dec 1 st, 24 sc (UK dc), dec 1 st, 3 sc (UK dc), dec 1 st, 3 sc (UK dc), dec 1 st (42 sts).

Rounds 31–33: 1 sc (UK dc) in each st of previous round (42 sts).

Round 34: dec 1 st, 2 sc (UK dc), dec 1 st, 2 sc (UK dc), dec 1 st, 22 sc (UK dc), dec 1 st, 2 sc (UK dc), dec 1 st, 2 sc (UK dc), dec 1 st (36 sts).

Rounds 35–37: 1 sc (UK dc) into each st of previous round (36 sts).

Round 38: dec 1 st, 1 sc (UK dc), dec 1 st, 1 sc (UK dc), dec st, 20 sc (UK dc), dec 1 st, 1 sc (UK dc), dec 1 st, 1 sc (UK dc), dec 1 st (30 sts).

Round 39: 1 sc (UK dc) into each st of previous round (30 sts).

Round 40: *3 sc (UK dc), dec 1 st*, rep from * to * five more times (24 sts).

Secure the yarn and fasten off. Lightly stuff the wing.

FINISHING OFF

Sew the last round of each leg to the side of the body at rounds 20–25 using whip stitch. Make sure that the inc in rounds 36 and 37 of the leg are facing forward. Using Orange yarn, backstitch the last round of the beak to the edge of the last round of the head. Sew the last round of the body to the underside of rounds 6–14 of the head using whip stitch. Sew an eye to each side of the head. Using White yarn, embroider two French knots to each eye. Sew two eyelashes in Black yarn beside each eye. Press the last round of each wing together, and sew around the edge using whip stitch at round 51 of the body.

ASIA

Timmy
THE TIGER

Timmy is a veritable genius on the computer. He and his friends spend their time coding programs and inventing apps. But occasionally his mum makes him go outside to get fresh air and play.

HEIGHT
★ Approx. 13in (33cm)

MATERIAL
★ Austermann Merino 160 (100% merino wool); 1 ball each of Clementine 242 and Black 202, and small amounts of White 201; 50g/174yd/160m
★ 2.5mm (B-1/UK 13) crochet hook
★ Toy stuffing
★ Tapestry needle

TIGER PATTERN
3 rounds Clementine yarn, 1 round Black yarn, rep from * to * continuously.

HEAD AND BODY
Work in rounds. At the end of each round, work 1 sl st into first st in round, 1 ch and turn.

Round 1: using Clementine yarn, work 6 sc (UK dc) into a magic ring (6 sts).

Round 2: inc 1 st six times (12 sts).

Round 3: *1 sc (UK dc), inc 1 st*, rep from * to * five more times (18 sts).

Round 4: *2 sc (UK dc), inc 1 st*, rep from * to * five more times (24 sts).

Change to Black yarn.

Round 5: 3 sc (UK dc), inc 1 st*, rep from * to * five more times (30 sts).

Change to Clementine yarn. Now continue working in the Tiger Pattern.

Round 6: *4 sc (UK dc), inc 1 st*, rep from * to * five more times (36 sts).

Round 7: *5 sc (UK dc), inc 1 st*, rep from * to * five more times (42 sts).

Round 8: *6 sc (UK dc), inc 1 st*, rep from * to * five more times (48 sts).

Round 9: *7 sc (UK dc), inc 1 st*, rep from * to * five more times (54 sts).

Round 10: *8 sc (UK dc), inc 1 st*, rep from * to * five more times (60 sts).

Round 11: *9 sc (UK dc), inc 1 st*, rep from * to * five more times (66 sts).

Round 12: *10 sc (UK dc), inc 1 st*, rep from * to * five more times (72 sts).

Rounds 13–29: 1 sc (UK dc) into each st of previous round (72 sts).

Round 30: *10 sc (UK dc), dec 1 st*, rep from * to * five more times (66 sts).

Round 31: *9 sc (UK dc), dec 1 st*, rep from * to * five more times (60 sts).

Round 32: *8 sc (UK dc), dec 1 st*, rep from * to * five more times (54 sts).

Round 33: *7 sc (UK dc), dec 1 st*, rep from * to * five more times (48 sts).

Round 34: *6 sc (UK dc), dec 1 st*, rep from * to * five more times (42 sts).

Round 35: *5 sc (UK dc), dec 1 st*, rep from * to * five more times (36 sts).

Stuff the head.

Round 36: *4 sc (UK dc), dec 1 st*, rep from * to * five more times (30 sts).

Round 37: *3 sc (UK dc), dec 1 st*, rep from * to * five more times (24 sts).

Round 38: 1 sc (UK dc) into each st of previous round (24 sts).

The head now transitions to the body.

Round 39: inc 1 st 24 times (48 sts).

Rounds 40–74: 1 sc (UK dc) into each st of previous round (48 sts).

Stuff the body.

Round 75: *6 sc (UK dc), dec 1 st*, rep from * to * five more times (42 sts).

Round 76: *5 sc (UK dc), dec 1 st*, rep from * to * five more times (36 sts).

Round 77: *4 sc (UK dc), dec 1 st*, rep from * to * five more times (30 sts).

Round 78: *3 sc (UK dc), dec 1 st*, rep from * to * five more times (24 sts).

Round 79: *2 sc (UK dc), dec 1 st*, rep from * to * five more times (18 sts).

Round 80: *1 sc (UK dc), dec 1 st*, rep from * to * five more times (12 sts).

Round 81: dec 1 st six times (6 sts).

Round 82: *skip 1 st, 1 sl st*, rep from * to * twice more (3 sts).

Secure the yarn and fasten off.

EYES (MAKE 2)
Round 1: using Black yarn, work 6 sc (UK dc) into a magic ring (6 sts). Join in a round with 1 sl st into the first st. Secure the yarn and fasten off.

EYE SPOTS (MAKE 2)
Work in rows. Work 1 ch at the end of each row and turn the work.

Row 1: work 5 ch in White yarn. 1 sc (UK dc) into second ch from hook, 2 sc (UK dc), 3 sc (UK dc) in 1 st. Continue working on the other side of the ch: 3 sc (UK dc) (9 sts).

Row 2: 3 sc (UK dc), inc 1 st three times, 3 sc (UK dc) (12 sts).

Row 3: 2 sc (UK dc) in 1 st, 3 hdc (UK htr), 2 hdc (UK htr) in 1 st four times, 3 hdc (UK htr), 2 sc (UK dc) in 1 st (18 sts).

Secure the yarn and fasten off.

NOSE
In this pattern, the colours change within a round. Crochet around the yarn not currently being used. At the end of each round, work 1 sl st into first st in round, 1 ch and turn.

Round 1: using Black yarn, work 6 sc (UK dc) into a magic ring (6 sts).

Round 2: 2 sc (UK dc), 2 dc (UK tr) in 1 st three times, 1 sc (UK dc) (9 sts).

Round 3: *2 sc (UK dc), inc 1 st*, rep from * to * twice more (12 sts).

Change to Clementine yarn.

Round 4: *1 sc (UK dc), inc 1 st*, rep from * to * five more times (18 sts).

Join White yarn.

Round 5: *2 sc (UK dc), inc 1 st*, rep from * to * once in White yarn, *2 sc (UK dc), inc 1 st*, rep from * to * three more times in Clementine yarn (24 sts).

Rounds 6 and 7: 8 sc (UK dc) in White yarn, 16 sc (UK dc) in Clementine yarn (24 sts).

Round 8: inc 1 st, 6 sc (UK dc), inc 1 st in White yarn, 3 sc (UK dc), inc 1 st, 4 sc (UK dc), inc 1 st, 4 sc (UK dc), inc 1 st, 2 sc (UK dc) in Clementine yarn (29 sts).

Secure the yarn and fasten off. Stuff the nose.

EARS (MAKE 2 WHITE AND 2 BLACK)

Work in rows. Work 1 ch at the end of each row and turn the work.

Row 1: work 11 ch. 1 sc (UK dc) into second ch from hook, and 1 sc (UK dc) into each remaining ch (10 sts).

Row 2: 1 sc (UK dc) in each st of previous row (10 sts).

Row 3: dec 1 st, 6 sc (UK dc), dec 1 st (8 sts).

Rows 4 and 5: 1 sc (UK dc) in each st of previous row (8 sts).

Row 6: dec 1 st, 4 sc (UK dc), dec 1 st (6 sts).

Row 7: 1 sc (UK dc) in each st of previous row (6 sts).

Row 8: dec 1 st, 2 sc (UK dc), dec 1 st (4 sts).

Row 9: 1 sc (UK dc) in each st of previous row (4 sts).

Row 10: dec 1 st twice (2 sts).

Row 11: dec 1 st (1 st).

Secure the yarn and fasten off.

Place on ear of each colour together, and using Black yarn work sc (UK dc) around to join. Do not work sc (UK dc) on ch edge.

LEGS (MAKE 2)

Work in rounds. Work 1 ch to turn at the beg of each round, and finish each round with 1 sl st in the first st of the round.

Round 1: using White yarn, work 9 ch, 1 sc (UK dc) into second ch from hook, 1 sc (UK dc) into each of next 6 ch, 3 sc (UK dc) into last ch. Continue working on the other side of the length of ch: 6 sc (UK dc), 2 sc (UK dc) into same ch with first st in (18 sts).

Round 2: inc 1 st, 4 sc (UK dc), 2 hdc (UK htr), 2 dc (UK tr) into 1 st three times, 2 hdc (UK htr), 4 sc (UK dc), inc 1 st twice (24 sts).

Round 3: 6 sc (UK dc), 2 hdc (UK htr), 2 dc (UK tr) into 1 st six times, 2 hdc (UK htr), 7 sc (UK dc), inc 1 st (31 sts).

Round 4: work into the back bar of the stitch only: 1 sc (UK dc) into each st of previous round (31 sts).

Change to Clementine yarn.

Round 5: 9 sc (UK dc), *1 spike sc (UK dc) into previous round, 1 sc (UK dc)*, rep from * to * five more times, 10 sc (UK dc) (31 sts).

Rounds 6 and 7: 1 sc (UK dc) into each st of previous round (31 sts).

Round 8: 6 sc (UK dc), work 2 dc (UK tr) tog eight times, 9 sc (UK dc) (23 sts).

Rounds 9–11: 1 sc (UK dc) into each st of previous round (23 sts).

Change to Black yarn.

Round 12: 1 sc (UK dc) into each st of previous round (23 sts).

Change to Clementine yarn. Now continue working in Tiger Pattern.

Round 13–30: 1 sc (UK dc) into each st of previous round (23 sts).

Secure the yarn and fasten off. Stuff the leg. Only lightly stuff the last five rounds.

PAWS (MAKE 2)

Work in rounds. At the end of each round, work 1 sl st into first st in round, 1 ch and turn.

Round 1: using White yarn, work 12 dc (UK tr) into a magic ring (12 sts).

Round 2: 3 ch (as the first dc (UK tr)), 1 dc (UK tr) into first st of previous round, 2 dc (UK tr) in 1 st three times, 1 dc (UK tr), 3 ch, 1 sl st into same st as last dc (UK tr), 7 sc (UK dc).

Change to Clementine yarn.

Round 3: work into the back bar of the stitch only: 1 sc (UK dc) into each ch of first dc (UK tr) of previous round, 1 sc (UK dc) into each st of previous round and into each ch of last dc (UK tr) in previous round, 1 sc (UK dc) into each remaining st (21 sts).

Round 4: 1 sc (UK dc) into each st of previous round (21 sts).

Round 5: *5 sc (UK dc), dec 1 st*, rep from * to * twice more (18 sts).

Round 6: *4 sc (UK dc), dec 1 st*, rep from * to * twice more (12 sts).

Round 7: dec 1 st six times (6 sts).

Round 8: *skip 1 st, 1 sl st*, rep from * to * twice more (3 sts).

Secure the yarn and fasten off.

ARMS (MAKE 2)

Work in spiral rounds. This means the rounds are not finished with a sl st, nor do you work a turning ch at the beg of a new round.

Using Clementine yarn work 8 ch, and close the ch with 1 sl st into first ch to make a ring (8 sts).

Round 1: 1 sc (UK dc) into each ch (8 sts).

Change to Black yarn.

Round 2: 1 sc (UK dc) into each st of previous round (8 sts).

Change to Clementine yarn. Now continue working in Tiger Pattern.

Rounds 3–26: 1 sc (UK dc) into each st of previous round (8 sts).

Secure the yarn and fasten off.

FINISHING OFF

Press the last round of the legs together, and sew to the sides of the body with whip stitch with the tips of the feet facing forward. Sew round 1 of the arms to rounds 3 and 4 of the paws, on the narrow side, using whip stitch. Press the last round of arms together and sew the edge to the sides of the body at round 39 using whip stitch. Sew an ear to each side of the head near the back, the white part facing forward. Sew the last round of the nose to rounds 21–31 of the head using mattress stitch. Sew the eye spots above the nose, and the eyes to the middle of the eye spots. Using White yarn, embroider two French knots onto each eye and sew two eyelashes beside each eye with Black yarn.

Shu Shu
THE PANDA

It takes years of training to become a sushi master. Shu Shu, though, is a natural talent, and qualified in only a few months in Japan. He now travels the world making sushi for the people he meets.

HEIGHT
★ Approx. 9in (23cm)

MATERIALS
★ Lang Yarns Merino 70 (98% merino wool, 2% polyester) 2 balls Black 70 and 1 ball Pa-Bianco White 01; 50g/76yd/70m
★ Austermann Merino 160 (100% merino wool) scraps of Black 202 and White 201; 50g/174yd/160m
★ 4mm (G-6/UK 8) and 2.5mm (B-1/UK 13) crochet hooks
★ Toy stuffing
★ Tapestry needle

HEAD
Work in spiral rounds. This means the rounds are not finished with a sl st, nor do you work a turning ch at the beg of a new round.

Round 1: using 4mm (G-6/UK 8) hook and Pa-Bianco White yarn, work 6 sc (UK dc) into a magic ring (6 sts).

Round 2: inc 1 st six times (12 sts).

Round 3: *1 sc (UK dc), inc 1 st*, rep from * to * five more times (18 sts).

Round 4: *2 sc (UK dc), inc 1 st*, rep from * to * five more times (24 sts).

Round 5: *3 sc (UK dc), inc 1 st*, rep from * to * five more times (30 sts).

Round 6: *4 sc (UK dc), inc 1 st*, rep from * to * five more times (36 sts).

Round 7: *5 sc (UK dc), inc 1 st*, rep from * to * five more times (42 sts).

Round 8: *6 sc (UK dc), inc 1 st*, rep from * to * five more times (48 sts).

Round 9: *7 sc (UK dc), inc 1 st*, rep from * to * five more times (54 sts).

Round 10: *8 sc (UK dc), inc 1 st*, rep from * to * five more times (60 sts).

Rounds 11 and 12: 1 sc (UK dc) into each st of previous round (60 sts)

Round 13: *9 sc (UK dc), inc 1 st*, rep from * to * five more times (66 sts).

Rounds 14–16: 1 sc (UK dc) into each st of previous round (66 sts).

Round 17: *9 sc (UK dc), dec 1 st*, rep from * to * five more times (60 sts).

Round 18: 1 sc (UK dc) into each st of previous round (60 sts).

Round 19: *8 sc (UK dc), dec 1 st*, rep from * to * five more times (54 sts).

Round 20: *7 sc (UK dc), dec 1 st*, rep from * to * five more times (48 sts).

Round 21: *6 sc (UK dc), dec 1 st*, rep from * to * five more times (42 sts).

Round 22: 1 sc (UK dc) into each st of previous round (42 sts).

Round 23: *5 sc (UK dc), dec 1 st*, rep from * to * five more times (36 sts).

Round 24: *4 sc (UK dc), dec 1 st*, rep from * to * five more times (30 sts).
Stuff the head.

Round 25: *3 sc (UK dc), dec 1 st*, rep from * to * five more times (24 sts).

Round 26: *2 sc (UK dc), dec 1 st*, rep from * to * five more times (18 sts).

Round 27: *1 sc (UK dc), dec 1 st*, rep from * to * five more times (12 sts).

Round 28: dec 1 st six times (6 sts).

Round 29: *skip 1 st, 1 sl st*, rep from * to * twice more (3 sts).
Secure the yarn and fasten off.

BODY
Work in spiral rounds. This means the rounds are not finished with a sl st, nor do you work a turning ch at the beg of a new round.

Round 1: using 4mm (G-6/UK 8) hook and Pa-Bianco White yarn, work 6 sc (UK dc) into a magic ring (6 sts).

Round 2: inc 1 st six times (12 sts).

Round 3: *1 sc (UK dc), inc 1 st*, rep from * to * five more times (18 sts).

Round 4: *2 sc (UK dc), inc 1 st*, rep from * to * five more times (24 sts).

Round 5: *3 sc (UK dc), inc 1 st*, rep from * to * five more times (30 sts).

Round 6: *4 sc (UK dc), inc 1 st*, rep from * to * five more times (36 sts).

Round 7: *5 sc (UK dc), inc 1 st*, rep from * to * five more times (42 sts).

Round 8: *6 sc (UK dc), inc 1 st*, rep from * to * five more times (48 sts).

Round 9: *7 sc (UK dc), inc 1 st*, rep from * to * five more times (54 sts).

Rounds 10–17: 1 sc (UK dc) into each st of previous round (54 sts).

Round 18: *16 sc (UK dc), dec 1 st*, rep from * to * twice more (51 sts).

Rounds 19–21: 1 sc (UK dc) into each st of previous round (51 sts).
Change to Black yarn.

Rounds 22–24: 1 sc (UK dc) into each st of previous round (51 sts).

Round 25: *15 sc (UK dc), dec 1 st*, rep from * to * twice more (48 sts).

Round 26: 1 sc (UK dc) into each st of previous round (48 sts).

Round 27: *6 sc (UK dc), dec 1 st*, rep from * to * five more times (42 sts).

Round 28: *5 sc (UK dc), dec 1 st*, rep from * to * five more times (36 sts).

Round 29: *4 sc (UK dc), dec 1 st*, rep from * to * five more times (30 sts).
Secure the yarn and fasten off. Stuff the body.

ARMS (MAKE 2)
Work in spiral rounds. This means the rounds are not finished with a sl st, nor do you work a turning ch at the beg of a new round.

Round 1: using 4mm (G-6/UK 8) hook and Black yarn, work 6 sc (UK dc) into a magic ring (6 sts).

Round 2: inc 1 st six times (12 sts).

Round 3: 1 sc (UK dc) into each st of previous round (12 sts).

Round 4: *1 sc (UK dc), inc 1 st*, rep from * to * five more times (18 sts).

Round 5: 1 sc (UK dc) into each st of previous round (18 sts).

Round 6: *5 sc (UK dc), inc 1 st*, rep from * to * twice more (21 sts).

Rounds 7–9: 1 sc (UK dc) into each st of previous round (21 sts).
Secure the yarn and fasten off. Stuff the arm.

LEGS (MAKE 2)

Work in spiral rounds. This means the rounds are not finished with a sl st, nor do you work a turning ch at the beg of a new round.

Round 1: using 4mm (G-6/UK 8) hook and Black yarn, work 6 sc (UK dc) into a magic ring (6 sts).

Round 2: inc 1 st six times (12 sts).

Round 3: *1 sc (UK dc), inc 1 st*, rep from * to * five more times (18 sts).

Round 4: work into the back bar of the stitch only: 9 sc (UK dc); into both bars of the stitch: 9 sc (UK dc) (18 sts).

Round 5: 12 sc (UK dc), inc 1 st, 1 sc (UK dc), inc 1 st, 3 sc (UK dc) (20 sts).

Rounds 6 and 7: 1 sc (UK dc) into each st of previous round (20 sts).

Round 8: 14 sc (UK dc), inc 1 st twice, 4 sc (UK dc) (22 sts).

Rounds 9–11: 1 sc (UK dc) into each st of previous round (22 sts).
Secure the yarn and fasten off. Stuff the leg.

EYE SPOTS (MAKE 2)

Work in rounds. At the end of each round, work 1 sl st into first st in round, 1 ch and turn.

Round 1: using 4mm (G-6/UK 8) hook and Black yarn, work 7 ch. 1 sc (UK dc) into second ch from hook, 4 hdc (UK htr), 3 sc (UK dc) in last ch, now continue working on the other side of the ch: 4 hdc (UK htr), 2 sc (UK dc) into same ch as first st (15 sts).

Round 2: inc 1 st, 2 hdc (UK htr) in 1 st, 2 dc (UK tr), 2 hdc (UK htr) in 1 st, 2 sc (UK dc) in 1 st three times, 2 hdc (UK htr) in 1 st, 2 dc (UK tr), 2 hdc (UK htr) in 1 st, 2 sc (UK dc) in 1 st twice (24 sts).
Secure the yarn and fasten off.

EARS (MAKE 2)

Work in spiral rounds. This means the rounds are not finished with a sl st, nor do you work a turning ch at the beg of a new round.

Round 1: using 4mm (G-6/UK 8) hook and Black yarn, work 6 sc (UK dc) into a magic ring (6 sts).

Round 2: inc 1 st six times (12 sts).

Rounds 3 and 4: 1 sc (UK dc) into each st of previous round (12 sts).
Secure the yarn and fasten off.

EYES (MAKE 2)

Work in rounds. At the end of each round, work 1 sl st into first st in round, 1 ch and turn.

Round 1: using 2.5mm (B-1/UK 13) hook and Black yarn, work 6 sc (UK dc) into a magic ring (6 sts).
Change to White yarn.

Round 2: inc 1 st six times (12 sts).
Secure the yarn and fasten off.

FINISHING OFF

Sew the last round of the body to the last round of the head. Tilt the head so the back is tilting down and the face pointing up slightly. Attach the eye spots by backstitching along round 2 to rounds 9–19 of the head. Sew an eye into the lower part of each eye spot, then, using White yarn, embroider two French knots to each eye. Sew the last round of each arm to the sides of the body at rounds 21–26 using whip stitch. Sew the last round of each leg to rounds 8–14 of the body using whip stitch. The 9 sts that you worked into the back post only of round 4 of the leg should face up. Using Black yarn, sew a few horizontal lines onto the head at round 15 between the eye spots for the nose. To make the mouth, use Black yarn and sew a vertical line from the nose and two diagonal lines at the bottom, like an arrow.

Mabel
THE ELEPHANT

A real elephant loves peanuts more than anything else! And Mabel is definitely a real elephant. Mabel loves them so much that she always has a large stash of them close by. After all, you have to be ready for anything.

HEIGHT
★ Approx. 6¼in (16cm)

MATERIALS
★ Lang Yarns Merino+ Color (100% merino wool); 2 balls of Blue/Grey 79; 100g/196yd/180m
★ Austermann Merino 160 (100% merino wool); scraps of Black 202 and White 201; 50g/174yd/160m
★ 3mm (D-3/UK 11) and 2.5mm (B-1/UK 13) crochet hooks
★ Toy stuffing
★ Tapestry needle

UPPER BODY
Work in rows. Work 1 ch at the end of each row and turn the work.

Start at the back of the elephant.

Row 1: using 3mm (D-3/UK 11) hook and Blue/Grey yarn, work 41 ch, 1 sc (UK dc) into second ch from hook and each remaining ch (40 sts).

Row 2: 12 sc (UK dc), inc 1 st, 3 sc (UK dc), inc 1 st, 2 sc (UK dc), inc 1 st, 2 sc (UK dc), inc 1 st, 3 sc (UK dc), inc 1 st, 12 sc (UK dc) (46 sts).

Row 3: 13 sc (UK dc), inc 1 st, 4 sc (UK dc), inc 1 st, 3 sc (UK dc), inc 1 st twice, 3 sc (UK dc), inc 1 st, 4 sc (UK dc), inc 1 st, 13 sc (UK dc) (52 sts).

Row 4: 14 sc (UK dc), inc 1 st, 5 sc (UK dc), inc 1 st, 4 sc (UK dc), inc 1 st twice, 4 sc (UK dc), inc 1 st, 5 sc (UK dc), inc 1 st, 14 sc (UK dc) (58 sts).

Row 5: 26 sc (UK dc), inc 1 st, 4 sc (UK dc), inc 1 st, 26 sc (UK dc) (60 sts).

Row 6: 28 sc (UK dc), inc 1 st, 2 sc (UK dc), inc 1 st, 28 sc (UK dc) (62 sts).

Row 7: 29 sc (UK dc), inc 1 st, 2 sc (UK dc), inc 1 st, 29 sc (UK dc) (64 sts).

Row 8: 1 sc (UK dc) into each st of previous row (64 sts).

Row 9: 30 sc (UK dc), inc 1 st, 2 sc (UK dc), inc 1 st, 30 sc (UK dc) (66 sts).

Row 10: 1 sc (UK dc) into each st of previous row (66 sts).

Row 11: 31 sc (UK dc), inc 1 st, 2 sc (UK dc), inc 1 st, 31 sc (UK dc) (68 sts).

Row 12: 1 sc (UK dc) into each st of previous row (68 sts).

Row 13: 32 sc (UK dc), inc 1 st, 2 sc (UK dc), inc 1 st, 32 sc (UK dc) (70 sts).

Row 14: 1 sc (UK dc) into each st of previous row (70 sts).

Secure the yarn and fasten off, then turn work. Now make the back legs. Join Blue/Grey yarn to the 11th st of the prev row, and continue working in rows:

Row 15: dec 1 st, 46 sc (UK dc), dec 1 st. Do not work the remaining st (48 sts).

Row 16: dec 1 st, 44 sc (UK dc), dec 1 st (46 sts).

Row 17: dec 1 st, 42 sc (UK dc), dec 1 st (44 sts).

Row 18: dec 1 st, 40 sc (UK dc), dec 1 st (42 sts).

Rows 19–23: 1 sc (UK dc) into each st of previous row (42 sts).

Row 24: inc 1 st, 40 sc (UK dc), inc 1 st (44 sts).

Row 25: inc 1 st, 42 sc (UK dc), inc 1 st (46 sts).

Row 26: inc 1 st, 44 sc (UK dc), inc 1 st (48 sts).

Row 27: inc 1 st, 46 sc (UK dc), inc 1 st (50 sts), 11 ch.

Turn the work as usual.

Now continue with the front legs:

Row 28: 1 sc (UK dc) into second ch from the hook, 1 sc (UK dc) into each of next 9 ch, 50 sc (UK dc). Turn the work. 11 ch, 1 sc (UK dc)* into second ch from hook, 1 sc (UK dc) into the remaining 9 ch, 1 sl st into last of 50 sc (UK dc) (70 sts).

Secure the yarn and fasten off. Join Blue/Grey yarn to the outer st of the row just worked (the st with the *) and continue as follows:

Rows 29–37: 1 sc (UK dc) into each st of previous row (70 sts).

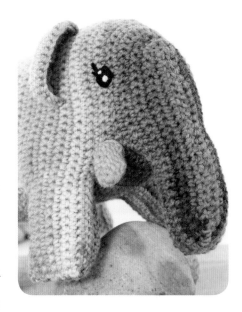

Secure the yarn and fasten off, then turn work as usual. Now work the head. Join Blue/Grey yarn to the 15th st of the prev row, and continue as follows:

Row 38: dec 1 st, 38 sc (UK dc), dec 1 st (40 sts).

Row 39: dec 1 st, 36 sc (UK dc), dec 1 st (38 sts).

Row 40: 11 sc (UK dc), dec 1 st, 1 sc (UK dc), dec 1 st, 1 sc (UK dc), dec 1 st twice, 1 sc (UK dc), dec 1 st, 1 sc (UK dc), dec 1 st, 11 sc (UK dc) (32 sts).

Row 41: 1 sc (UK dc) in each st of previous row (32 sts), 17 ch.

Turn the work as usual. Now work the trunk.

Row 42: 1 sc (UK dc) into second ch from the hook, 1 sc (UK dc) into the remaining 15 ch, 32 sc (UK dc). Turn the work. 17 ch, 1 sc (UK dc)* into second ch from hook, 1 sc (UK dc) into remaining 15 ch, 1 sl st into last of 32 sts (64 sts).

Secure the yarn and fasten off.

Join Blue/Grey yarn to the outer st of the row just worked (the st with the *) and work the trunk:

Row 43: 1 sc (UK dc) into each st of previous row (64 sts).

Row 15: inc 1 st, 2 sc (UK dc), inc 1 st (6 sts).

Row 16: 1 sc (UK dc) into each st of previous row (6 sts).

Row 17: inc 1 st, 4 sc (UK dc), inc 1 st (8 sts).

Rows 18–23: 1 sc (UK dc) into each st of previous row (8 sts). Work 15 ch after row 23. Turn the work as usual, then continue as follows for the front legs:

Row 24: 1 sc (UK dc) into second ch from hook, 1 sc (UK dc) into the remaining 13 ch, 8 sc (UK dc). Turn the work. 15 ch, 1 sc (UK dc)* into second ch from hook, 1 sc (UK dc) into the remaining 13 ch, 1 sl st into last st in row 23 (36 sts).

Secure the yarn and fasten off. Join Blue/Grey yarn to the outer st of the row just worked (the st with the *) and continue as follows:

Rows 25–33: 1 sc (UK dc) into each st of previous row (36 sts).

Secure the yarn and fasten off. Turn the work. For the tummy, join Blue/Grey yarn to the 11th st of row 33, and continue working as follows:

Row 34: 16 sc (UK dc). Do not work the remaining st (16 sts).

Rows 35–45: 1 sc (UK dc) into each st of previous row (16 sts).

Work 11 ch after row 45. Turn the work as usual, then continue as follows for the back legs:

Row 46: 1 sc (UK dc) into second ch from hook, 1 sc (UK dc) into the remaining 9 ch, 16 sc (UK dc). Turn the work. 11 ch, 1 sc (UK dc)* into second ch from hook, 1 sc (UK dc) into the remaining 9 ch, 1 sl st into last st in the row 45 (36 sts).

Secure the yarn and fasten off. Join Blue/Grey yarn to the outer st of the row just worked (the st with the *) and continue as follows:

Rows 47–55: 1 sc (UK dc) into each st of previous row (36 sts).

Row 44: 26 sc (UK dc), dec 1 st six times, 26 sc (UK dc) (58 sts).

Row 45: dec 1 st, 54 sc (UK dc), dec 1 st (56 sts).

Row 46: dec 1 st, 52 sc (UK dc), dec 1 st (54 sts).

Row 47: dec 1 st, 23 sc (UK dc), dec 1 st twice, 23 sc (UK dc), dec 1 st (50 sts).

Row 48: dec 1 st, 21 sc (UK dc), dec 1 st twice, 21 sc (UK dc), dec 1 st (46 sts).

Row 49: dec 1 st, 19 sc (UK dc), dec 1 st twice, 19 sc (UK dc), dec 1 st (42 sts).

Secure the yarn and fasten off leaving a long tail.

LOWER BODY

Work in rows. Work 1 ch at the end of each row and turn the work.

Start with the elephant's trunk.

Row 1: using 3mm (D-3/UK 11) hook and Blue/Grey yarn, work 3 ch, 1 sc (UK dc) into second ch from the hook and in each further ch (2 sts).

Row 2: inc 1 st twice (4 sts).

Rows 3–14: 1 sc (UK dc) into each st of previous row (4 sts).

Secure the yarn and fasten off. Turn the work as usual. Join Blue/Grey yarn to the 16th st of row 55 and continue crocheting as follows:

Row 56: 6 sc (UK dc). Do not work the remaining st (6 sts).

Row 57: dec 1 st, 2 sc (UK dc), dec 1 st (4 sts).

Row 58: 1 sc (UK dc) into each st of previous row (4 sts).

Row 59: dec 1 st twice (2 sts).

Row 60: dec 1 st (1 st).

Secure the yarn and fasten off, leaving a long tail.

FEET (MAKE 2)

Work in rounds. At the end of each round, work 1 sl st into first st in round, 1 ch and turn.

Round 1: using 3mm (D-3/UK 11) hook and Blue/Grey yarn, work 6 sc (UK dc) into a magic ring (6 sts).

Round 2: inc 1 st six times (12 sts).

Round 3: *1 sc (UK dc), inc 1 st*, rep from * to * five more times (18 sts).

Round 4: *2 sc (UK dc), inc 1 st*, rep from * to * five more times (24 sts).

Secure the yarn and fasten off.

EARS (MAKE 2)

Work in rounds. At the end of each round, work 1 sl st into first st in round, 1 ch and turn.

Round 1: using 3mm (D-3/UK 11) hook and Blue/Grey yarn, work 3 sc (UK dc) into a magic ring (3 sts).

Round 2: inc 1 st three times (6 sts).

Round 3: *1 sc (UK dc), inc 1 st*, rep from * to * twice more (9 sts).

Round 4: *2 sc (UK dc), inc 1 st*, rep from * to * twice more (12 sts).

Round 5: *3 sc (UK dc), inc 1 st*, rep from * to * twice more (15 sts).

Round 6: *4 sc (UK dc), inc 1 st*, rep from * to * twice more (18 sts).

Rounds 7 and 8: 1 sc (UK dc) into each st of previous round (18 sts).

Secure the yarn and fasten off.

TUSKS (MAKE 2)

Work in spiral rounds. This means the rounds are not finished with a sl st, nor do you work a turning ch at the beg of a new round.

Round 1: using 3mm (D-3/UK 11) hook and Blue/Grey yarn, work 3 sc (UK dc) into a magic ring (3 sts).

Round 2: inc 1 st three times (6 sts).

Round 3: 1 sc (UK dc) into each st of previous round (6 sts).

Round 4: *1 sc (UK dc), inc 1 st*, rep from * to * twice more (9 sts).

Rounds 5–7: 1 sc (UK dc) into each st of previous round (9 sts).

Secure yarn and fasten off.

EYES (MAKE 2)

Round 1: using 2.5mm (B-1/UK 13) hook and Black yarn, work 6 sc (UK dc) into a magic ring (6 sts).

Join in a round with 1 sl st into the first st. Secure the yarn and fasten off.

FINISHING OFF

Fold the last row of the lower body to the middle, and sew the edges together with whip stitch. Sew the ends of the last 8 rows of the upper body together (trunk), again in whip stitch. Place the two parts of the body together so the front and back legs are completely aligned. Only sew the sides of the back legs together, leaving an opening at the foot. Sew the feet onto these openings using mattress stitch. Place the trunk part of the lower body into the remaining opening for the trunk on the upper body. Pin the two pieces of work together. Sew along the edges of the two body parts in mattress stitch. Stuff the elephant before sewing up. Sew an ear to either side of the elephant's head aligned with the front legs. Sew the last round of the tusks between the trunk and the front leg using whip stitch. Sew an eye to each side of the head above the tusk. Using White yarn, embroider two French knots to each eye. Using Black yarn, sew two eyelashes beside each eye.

AUSTRALIA

Jimmy
THE KOALA

Koalas are usually quite chilled and laid back, but Jimmy is full of energy. Fortunately his siblings are also energetic, so they have the best adventures together as they run around the outback.

HEIGHT
★ Approx. 10½in (27cm)

MATERIALS
★ Lang Yarns Merino 70 Dégradé (98% merino wool, 2% polyester); 2 balls of Grey/Berry 0066; 100g/153yd/140m
★ Lang Yarns Merino 70 (98% merino wool, 2% polyester); 1 ball each of White 0094 and Mélange Anthracite 0070; 50g/76yd/70m
★ 4mm (G-6/UK 8) crochet hook
★ Toy stuffing
★ Tapestry needle

HEAD
Work in spiral rounds. This means the rounds are not finished with a sl st, nor do you work a turning ch at the beg of a new round.

Round 1: using Grey/Berry yarn, work 6 sc (UK dc) into a magic ring (6 sts).

Round 2: inc 1 st six times (12 sts).

Round 3: *1 sc (UK dc), inc 1 st*, rep from * to * five more times (18 sts).

Round 4: *2 sc (UK dc), inc 1 st*, rep from * to * five more times (24 sts).

Round 5: *3 sc (UK dc), inc 1 st*, rep from * to * five more times (30 sts).

Round 6: *4 sc (UK dc), inc 1 st*, rep from * to * five more times (36 sts).

Round 7: *5 sc (UK dc), inc 1 st*, rep from * to * five more times (42 sts).

Round 8: *6 sc (UK dc), inc 1 st*, rep from * to * five more times (48 sts).

Round 9: *7 sc (UK dc), inc 1 st*, rep from * to * five more times (54 sts).

Round 10: *8 sc (UK dc), inc 1 st*, rep from * to * five more times (60 sts).

Rounds 11–17: 1 sc (UK dc) into each st of previous round (60 sts).

Round 18: *8 sc (UK dc), dec 1 st*, rep from * to * five more times (54 sts).

Round 19: *7 sc (UK dc), dec 1 st*, rep from * to * five more times (48 sts).

Rounds 20–24: 1 sc (UK dc) into each st of previous round (48 sts).

Round 25: *6 sc (UK dc), dec 1 st*, rep from * to * five more times (42 sts). Stuff the head.

Round 26: 1 sc (UK dc) into each st of previous round (42 sts).

Round 27: *5 sc (UK dc), dec 1 st*, rep from * to * five more times (36 sts).

Round 28: 1 sc (UK dc) into each st of previous round (36 sts).

Round 29: *4 sc (UK dc), dec 1 st*, rep from * to * five more times (30 sts).

Round 30: *3 sc (UK dc), dec 1 st*, rep from * to * five more times (24 sts).

Round 31: *2 sc (UK dc), dec 1 st*, rep from * to * five more times (18 sts).

Round 32: *1 sc (UK dc), dec 1 st*, rep from * to * five more times (12 sts).

Round 33: dec 1 st six times (6 sts).

Round 34: *skip 1 st, 1 sl st*, rep from * to * twice more (3 sts).
Secure the yarn and fasten off.

BODY
Work in spiral rounds. This means the rounds are not finished with a sl st, nor do you work a turning ch at the beg of a new round.

Round 1: using Grey/Berry yarn, work 6 sc (UK dc) into a magic ring (6 sts).

Round 2: inc 1 st six times (12 sts).

Round 3: *1 sc (UK dc), inc 1 st*, rep from * to * five more times (18 sts).

Round 4: *2 sc (UK dc), inc 1 st*, rep from * to * five more times (24 sts).

Round 5: *3 sc (UK dc), inc 1 st*, rep from * to * five more times (30 sts).

Round 6: *4 sc (UK dc), inc 1 st*, rep from * to * five more times (36 sts).

Round 7: *5 sc (UK dc), inc 1 st*, rep from * to * five more times (42 sts).

Round 8: *6 sc (UK dc), inc 1 st*, rep from * to * five more times (48 sts).

Round 9: *7 sc (UK dc), inc 1 st*, rep from * to * five more times (54 sts).

Rounds 10–20: 1 sc (UK dc) into each st of previous round (54 sts).

Round 21: *7 sc (UK dc), dec 1 st*, rep from * to * five more times (48 sts).

Round 22: *6 sc (UK dc), dec 1 st*, rep from * to * five more times (42 sts).

Round 23: *5 sc (UK dc), dec 1 st*, rep from * to * five more times (36 sts).
Secure the yarn and fasten off. Stuff the body.

LEGS (MAKE 2)
Work in spiral rounds. This means the rounds are not finished with a sl st, nor do you work a turning ch at the beg of a new round.

Round 1: using Mélange Anthracite yarn, work 6 sc (UK dc) into a magic ring (6 sts).

Round 2: inc 1 st six times (12 sts).

Round 3: *1 sc (UK dc), inc 1 st*, rep from * to * five more times (18 sts).

Round 4: 1 sc (UK dc) into each st of previous round (18 sts).
Change to Grey/Berry yarn.

Rounds 5–13: 1 sc (UK dc) into each st of previous round (18 sts).

NOSE

Work in rounds. At the end of each round, work 1 sl st into first st in round, 1 ch and turn.

Round 1: using Mélange Anthracite yarn, work 5 ch, 1 sc (UK dc) into second ch from hook, 1 sc (UK dc) into each of next 2 ch, 3 sc (UK dc) into last ch. Continue working on the other side of the length of ch: 2 sc (UK dc), 2 sc (UK dc) into the same ch as the first st (10 sts).

Round 2: 4 sc (UK dc), 3 sc (UK dc) in 1 st, 4 sc (UK dc), 3 sc (UK dc) in 1 st (14 sts).

Round 3: 6 sc (UK dc), inc 1 st, 7 sc (UK dc) (15 sts).

Round 4: 5 sc (UK dc), inc 1 st, 2 sc (UK dc), inc 1 st, 6 sc (UK dc) (17 sts).

Secure the yarn and fasten off. Stuff the nose.

MOUTH

Work in rounds. At the end of each round, work 1 sl st into first st in round, 1 ch and turn.

Round 1: using White yarn, work following st into a magic ring: 2 sc (UK dc), 1 hdc (UK htr), 3 dc (UK tr), 1 hdc (UK htr), 6 sc (UK dc) (13 sts).

Round 2: 1 sc (UK dc), 1 hdc (UK htr), 1 dc (UK tr), 2 dc (UK tr) in 1 st, 3 dc (UK tr) in 1 st, 2 dc (UK tr) in 1 st, 1 dc (UK tr), 1 hdc (UK htr), 5 sc (UK dc) (17 sts).

Round 3: 1 sc (UK dc), 1 hdc (UK htr), [3 dc (UK tr), 1 ch, 3 dc (UK htr)] in 1 st, 3 dc (UK tr), [3 dc (UK tr), 1 ch, 3 dc (UK tr)] in 1 st, 3 dc (UK tr), [3 dc (UK tr), 1 ch, 3 dc (UK tr)] in 1 st, 1 hdc (UK htr), 5 sc (UK dc) (23 sts).

Round 4: 1 sc (UK dc) into each st of previous round (23 sts).

Secure the yarn and fasten off leaving a long tail.

Secure the yarn and fasten off. Stuff the leg as far as round 11.

ARMS (MAKE 2)

Work in spiral rounds. This means the rounds are not finished with a sl st, nor do you work a turning ch at the beg of a new round.

Round 1: using Mélange Anthracite yarn, work 6 sc (UK dc) into a magic ring (6 sts).

Round 2: inc 1 st six times (12 sts).

Round 3: 1 sc (UK dc) into each st of previous round (12 sts).

Change to Grey/Berry yarn.

Rounds 4 and 5: 1 sc (UK dc) into each st of previous round (12 sts).

Rounds 6: *3 sc (UK dc), inc 1 st*, rep from * to * twice more (15 sts).

Rounds 7 and 8: 1 sc (UK dc) into each st of previous round (15 sts).

Round 9: *4 sc (UK dc), inc 1 st*, rep from * to * twice more (18 sts).

Rounds 10–13: 1 sc (UK dc) into each st of previous round (18 sts).

Secure the yarn and fasten off. Stuff the arm as far as round 11.

EARS (MAKE 2)

Work in rounds. At the end of each round, work 1 sl st into first st in round, 1 ch and turn.

Round 1: using White yarn, work 6 sc (UK dc) into a magic ring (6 sts).

Round 2: 1 sc (UK dc) into each st of previous round (6 sts).

Round 3: inc 1 st six times (12 sts).

Round 4: 1 sc (UK dc) into each st of previous round (12 sts).

Round 5: *1 sc (UK dc), inc 1 st*, rep from * to * five more times (18 sts).

Round 6: *2 sc (UK dc), inc 1 st*, rep from * to * five more times (24 sts).

Change to Grey/Berry yarn.

Round 7: work into the back bar of the stitch only: 1 sc (UK dc) into each st of previous round (24 sts).

Round 8: 1 sc (UK dc) into each st of previous round (24 sts).

Round 9: *2 sc (UK dc), dec 1 st*, rep from * to * five more times (18 sts).

Round 10: *1 sc (UK dc), dec 1 st*, rep from * to * five more times (12 sts).

Round 11: 1 sc (UK dc) into each st of previous round (12 sts).

Round 12: dec 1 st six times (6 sts).

Round 13: *skip 1 st, 1 sl st*, rep from * to * twice more (3 sts).

Secure the yarn and fasten off. Push the white part into the part in Grey/Berry yarn.

BORDERS (MAKE 2)

Join White yarn to the front bar of any st in round 6 of the ear, and work the following:

1 ch, 1 sl st into next st, *1 sl st, 3 ch, 1 sl st into next st*, rep from * to * twice more, 1 sl st, 2 ch, 1 sl st. Secure the yarn and fasten off.

LEFT EYE

Work in rounds. At the end of each round, work 1 sl st into first st in round, 1 ch and turn.

Round 1: using Mélange Anthracite yarn, work 6 sc (UK dc) into a magic ring (6 sts). Change to White yarn.

Round 2: [1 sl st and 1 sc (UK dc)] in 1 st, 2 dc (UK tr) in 1 st twice, [1 dc (UK tr) and 1 hdc (UK htr)] in 1 st, [2 sc (UK dc) and 1 sl st] in 1 st.

Secure the yarn and fasten off.

RIGHT EYE

Work in rounds. At the end of each round, work 1 sl st into first st in round, 1 ch and turn.

Round 1: using Mélange Anthracite yarn, work 6 sc (UK dc) into a magic ring (6 sts). Change to White yarn.

Round 2: 2 sc (UK dc) in 1 st, [1 hdc (UK htr) and 1 dc (UK tr)] in 1 st, 2 dc (UK tr) in 1 st twice, [1 sc (UK dc) and 1 sl st] in 1 st.

Secure the yarn and fasten off.

FINISHING OFF

Sew the last round of the body to the first round of the head at a slight angle so the koala looks up slightly when upright. Use whip stitch to sew the last round of each arm to rounds 16–23 of the body, also at a slight angle and with the magic rings of both arms facing forward. Use whip stitch to sew the last round of each leg to the sides of the body at rounds 5–12, almost horizontal, with the magic rings of both legs facing forward. Secure the insides of the legs to the body with a few stitches. Use backstitch to sew the last round of the mouth to the lower half of the front of the head. Sew the nose (with the inc of rounds 3 and 4 pointing down) to the head and so it partly overlaps the mouth. Use backstitch to sew the eyes to the left and right of the nose. Using White yarn, embroider two French knots onto the pupils of each eye. Sew the ears to rows 23–27 at the sides of the head. Ensure that the border is pointing upwards and outwards at an angle.

Marsha
THE KANGAROO

Marsha is a real cuddlebug - and a great boxer. Like all kangaroos she loves going to the gym to workout, and bounces her way through all the exercise classes. That way she's super strong for her next boxing match.

Let's Go

HEIGHT
★ Approx. 12¼in (31cm)

MATERIAL
★ Lang Yarns Merino+ Color (100% merino wool); 2 balls of Orange/Mixed 0059; 100g/196yd/180m
★ Austermann Merino 160 (100% merino wool); scraps of Black 202 and White 201; 50g/174yd/160m
★ 3mm (D-3/UK 11) and 2.5mm (B-1/UK 13) crochet hooks
★ Toy stuffing
★ Tapestry needle

HEAD
Work in spiral rounds. This means the rounds are not finished with a sl st, nor do you work a turning ch at the beg of a new round.

Round 1: using 3mm (D-3/UK 11) hook and Orange/Mixed yarn, work 6 sc (UK dc) into a magic ring (6 sts).
Round 2: inc 1 st six times (12 sts).
Round 3: *1 sc (UK dc), inc 1 st*, rep from * to * five more times (18 sts).
Round 4: *2 sc (UK dc), inc 1 st*, rep from * to * five more times (24 sts).
Round 5: 1 sc (UK dc) into each st of previous round (24 sts).
Round 6: *3 sc (UK dc), inc 1 st*, rep from * to * five more times (30 sts).
Rounds 7 and 8: 1 sc (UK dc) into each st of previous round (30 sts).
Round 9: *4 sc (UK dc), inc 1 st*, rep from * to * five more times (36 sts).
Rounds 10–12: 1 sc (UK dc) into each st of previous round (36 sts).
Round 13: *5 sc (UK dc), inc 1 st*, rep from * to * five more times (42 sts).
Rounds 14–20: 1 sc (UK dc) into each st of previous round (42 sts).

Round 21: *5 sc (UK dc), dec 1 st*, rep from * to * five more times (36 sts). Stuff the head.
Round 22: *4 sc (UK dc), dec 1 st*, rep from * to * five more times (30 sts).
Round 23: *3 sc (UK dc), dec 1 st*, rep from * to * five more times (24 sts).
Round 24: *2 sc (UK dc), dec 1 st*, rep from * to * five more times (18 sts).
Round 25: *1 sc (UK dc), dec 1 st*, rep from * to * five more times (12 sts).
Round 26: dec 1 st six times (6 sts).
Round 27: *skip 1 st, 1 sl st*, rep from * to * twice more (3 sts).
Secure the yarn and fasten off.

BODY
Work in spiral rounds. This means the rounds are not finished with a sl st, nor do you work a turning ch at the beg of a new round.

Round 1: using 3mm (D-3/UK 11) hook and Orange/Mixed yarn, work 6 sc (UK dc) into a magic ring (6 sts).
Round 2: inc 1 st six times (12 sts).
Round 3: *1 sc (UK dc), inc 1 st*, rep from * to * five more times (18 sts).
Round 4: *2 sc (UK dc), inc 1 st*, rep from * to * five more times (24 sts).
Round 5: *3 sc (UK dc), inc 1 st*, rep from * to * five more times (30 sts).
Round 6: *4 sc (UK dc), inc 1 st*, rep from * to * five more times (36 sts).
Round 7: *5 sc (UK dc), inc 1 st*, rep from * to * five more times (42 sts).
Round 8: *6 sc (UK dc), inc 1 st*, rep from * to * five more times (48 sts).
Round 9: *7 sc (UK dc), inc 1 st*, rep from * to * five more times (54 sts).
Round 10: *8 sc (UK dc), inc 1 st*, rep from * to * five more times (60 sts).
Round 11: *9 sc (UK dc), inc 1 st*, rep from * to * five more times (66 sts).
Round 12: *10 sc (UK dc), inc 1 st*, rep from * to * five more times (72 sts).
Rounds 13–18: 1 sc (UK dc) into each st of previous round (72 sts).

Round 19: *10 sc (UK dc), dec 1 st*, rep from * to * five more times (66 sts).
Round 20: *9 sc (UK dc), dec 1 st*, rep from * to * five more times (60 sts).
Rounds 21–25: 1 sc (UK dc) into each st of previous round (60 sts).
Round 26: *8 sc (UK dc), dec 1 st*, rep from * to * five more times (54 sts).
Rounds 27–29: 1 sc (UK dc) into each st of previous round (54 sts).
Round 30: *7 sc (UK dc), dec 1 st*, rep from * to * five more times (48 sts).
Rounds 31–33: 1 sc (UK dc) into each st of previous round (48 sts).
Round 34: *6 sc (UK dc), dec 1 st*, rep from * to * five more times (42 sts).
Stuff the body.

Rounds 35 and 36: 1 sc (UK dc) into each st of previous round (42 sts).

Round 37: *5 sc (UK dc), dec 1 st*, rep from * to * five more times (36 sts).

Round 38: 1 sc (UK dc) into each st of previous round (36 sts).

Round 39: *4 sc (UK dc), dec 1 st*, rep from * to * five more times (30 sts).

Round 40: 1 sc (UK dc) into each st of previous round (36 sts).

Round 41: *3 sc (UK dc), dec 1 st*, rep from * to * five more times (24 sts).

Round 42: 1 sc (UK dc) into each st of previous round (36 sts).

Round 43: *2 sc (UK dc), dec 1 st*, rep from * to * five more times (18 sts).

Round 44: *1 sc (UK dc), dec 1 st*, rep from * to * five more times (12 sts).

Secure the yarn and fasten off. Add a little more stuffing.

ARMS (MAKE 2)

Work in spiral rounds. This means the rounds are not finished with a sl st, nor do you work a turning ch at the beg of a new round.

Round 1: using 3mm (D-3/UK 11) hook and Orange/Mixed yarn, work 6 sc (UK dc) into a magic ring (6 sts).

Round 2: inc 1 st six times (12 sts).

Rounds 3–5: 1 sc (UK dc) into each st of previous round (12 sts).

Round 6: *2 sc (UK dc), dec 1 st*, rep from * to * twice more (9 sts).

Round 7: *1 sc (UK dc), dec 1 st*, rep from * to * twice more (6 sts).

Rounds 8–25: 1 sc (UK dc) into each st of previous round (6 sts).

Secure the yarn and fasten off. Do not stuff the arm.

LEGS (MAKE 2)
PART 1

Work in spiral rounds. This means the rounds are not finished with a sl st, nor do you work a turning ch at the beg of a new round.

Round 1: using 3mm (D-3/UK 11) hook and Orange/Mixed yarn, work 6 sc (UK dc) into a magic ring (6 sts).

Round 2: inc 1 st six times (12 sts).

Rounds 3–20: 1 sc (UK dc) into each st of previous round (12 sts).

Secure the yarn and fasten off. Stuff Part 1 of the leg.

PART 2

Work in spiral rounds. This means the rounds are not finished with a sl st, nor do you work a turning ch at the beg of a new round.

Round 1: using 3mm (D-3/UK 11) hook and Orange/Mixed yarn, work 6 sc (UK dc) into a magic ring (6 sts).

Round 2: inc 1 st six times (12 sts).

Rounds 3–10: 1 sc (UK dc) into each st of previous round (12 sts).

Round 11: *3 sc (UK dc), inc 1 st*, rep from * to * twice more (15 sts).

Round 12: 1 sc (UK dc) into each st of previous round (15 sts).

Round 13: *4 sc (UK dc), inc 1 st*, rep from * to * twice more (18 sts).

Round 14: 1 sc (UK dc) into each st of previous round (18 sts).

Round 15: *2 sc (UK dc), inc 1 st*, rep from * to * five more times (24 sts).

Round 16: 1 sc (UK dc) into each st of previous round (24 sts).

Round 17: *3 sc (UK dc), inc 1 st*, rep from * to * five more times (30 sts).

Round 18: 1 sc (UK dc) into each st of previous round (30 sts).

Round 19: *4 sc (UK dc), inc 1 st*, rep from * to * five more times (36 sts).

Round 20: 1 sc (UK dc) into each st of previous round (36 sts).

Round 21: *5 sc (UK dc), inc 1 st*, rep from * to * five more times (42 sts).

Round 22: 1 sc (UK dc) into each st of previous round (42 sts).

Round 23: *6 sc (UK dc), inc 1 st*, rep from * to * five more times (48 sts).

Secure the yarn and fasten off. Stuff Part 2 of the leg as far as round 20. Using whip stitch sew the last round of Part 1 with to the side of the first six rounds of Part 2.

TAIL

Work in spiral rounds. This means the rounds are not finished with a sl st, nor do you work a turning ch at the beg of a new round.

Round 1: using 3mm (D-3/UK 11) hook and Orange/Mixed yarn, work 3 sc (UK dc) into a magic ring (3 sts).

Round 2: inc 1 st three times (6 sts).

Round 3: 1 sc (UK dc) into each st of previous round (6 sts).

Round 4: *1 sc (UK dc), inc 1 st*, rep from * to * twice more (9 sts).

Rounds 5–7: 1 sc (UK dc) into each st of previous round (9 sts).

Round 8: *2 sc (UK dc), inc 1 st* rep from * to * twice more (12 sts).

Rounds 9 and 10: 1 sc (UK dc) into each st of previous round (12 sts).

Round 11: *3 sc (UK dc), inc 1 st*, rep from * to * twice more (15 sts).

Rounds 12 and 13: 1 sc (UK dc) into each st of previous round (15 sts).

Round 14: *4 sc (UK dc), inc 1 st*, rep from * to * twice more (18 sts).

Round 15: *5 sc (UK dc), inc 1 st*, rep from * to * twice more (21 sts).

Round 16: 1 sc (UK dc) into each st of previous round (21 sts).

Round 17: 5 sc (UK dc), inc 1 st, 1 sc (UK dc), inc 1 st, 13 sc (UK dc) (23 sts).

Round 18: 1 sc (UK dc) into each st of previous row (23 sts).

Round 19: 6 sc (UK dc), inc 1 st, 1 sc (UK dc), inc 1 st, 14 sc (UK dc) (25 sts).

Round 20: 1 sc (UK dc) into each st of previous round (25 sts).

Round 21: 6 sc (UK dc), inc 1 st, 5 sc (UK dc), inc 1 st, 12 sc (UK dc) (27 sts).

Rounds 22 and 23: 1 sc (UK dc) into each st of previous round (27 sts).

Round 24: 7 sc (UK dc), inc 1 st, 2 sc (UK dc), inc 1 st, 3 sc (UK dc), inc 1 st, 12 sc (UK dc) (30 sts).

Round 25: 1 sc (UK dc) into each st of previous round (30 sts).

Round 26: *4 sc (UK dc), inc 1 st*, rep from * to * five more times (36 sts).

Rounds 27 and 28: 1 sc (UK dc) into each st of previous round (36 sts).

Round 29: 8 sc (UK dc), inc 1 st, 5 sc (UK dc), inc 1 st, 5 sc (UK dc), inc 1 st, 15 sc (UK dc) (39 sts).

Round 30: 9 sc (UK dc), inc 1 st, 6 sc (UK dc), inc 1 st, 6 sc (UK dc), inc 1 st, 15 sc (UK dc) (42 sts).

Round 31: 1 sc (UK dc) into each st of previous round (42 sts).

Round 32: 7 sc (UK dc), inc 1 st, 9 sc (UK dc), inc 1 st, 10 sc (UK dc), inc 1 st, 13 sc (UK dc) (45 sts).

Secure yarn and fasten off. Stuff the tail.

POUCH

Work in rows. Work 1 ch at the end of each row and turn the work.

Row 1: using 3mm (D-3/UK 11) hook and Orange/Mixed yarn, work 3 sc (UK dc) into a magic ring (3 sts).

Row 2: inc 1 st three times (6 sts).

Row 3: *1 sc (UK dc), inc 1 st*, rep from * to * twice more (9 sts).

Row 4: *2 sc (UK dc), inc 1 st*, rep from * to * twice more (12 sts).

Row 5: *3 sc (UK dc), inc 1 st*, rep from * to * twice more (15 sts).

Row 6: *4 sc (UK dc), inc 1 st*, rep from * to * twice more (18 sts).

Row 7: *5 sc (UK dc), inc 1 st*, rep from * to * twice more (21 sts).

Row 8: *6 sc (UK dc), inc 1 st*, rep from * to * twice more (24 sts).

Row 9: *7 sc (UK dc), inc 1 st*, rep from * to * twice more (27 sts).

Row 10: 1 sc (UK dc) into each st of previous row (27 sts).

Row 11: *8 sc (UK dc), inc 1 st*, rep from * to * twice more (30 sts).

Rows 12–14: 1 sc (UK dc) in each st of previous row (30 sts).

Secure the yarn and fasten off.

EYES (MAKE 2)

Round 1: using 2.5mm (B-1/UK 13) hook and Black yarn, work 6 sc (UK dc) into a magic ring (6 sts). Join in a round with 1 sl st into the first st. Secure the yarn and fasten off.

EARS (MAKE 2)

Work in rounds. At the end of each round, work 1 sl st into first st in round, 1 ch and turn.

Round 1: using 3mm (D-3/UK 11) hook and Orange/Mixed yarn, work 9 ch, 1 sc (UK dc) into second ch from hook, 1 hdc (UK htr), 3 dc (UK tr), 1 hdc (UK htr), 1 sc (UK dc), 3 sc (UK dc) in last ch. Continue working on the other side of the length of ch: 1 sc (UK dc), 1 hdc (UK htr), 3 dc (UK tr), 1 hdc (UK htr), 2 sc (UK dc) in same ch as first st (18 sts).

Round 2: 1 sc (UK dc), 1 hdc (UK htr), 3 dc (UK tr), 1 hdc (UK htr), 2 sc (UK dc), 3 sc (UK dc) in 1st, 2 sc (UK dc), 1 hdc (UK htr), 3 dc (UK tr), 1 hdc (UK htr), 2 sc (UK dc) (20 sts).

Secure the yarn and fasten off.

FINISHING OFF

Sew an ear (the side with the first st) to each side of the back of the head. Sew the eyes to the middle of the head. Using White yarn, embroider two French knots to each eye. In Black yarn, sew two eyelashes beside each eye. Using mattress stitch, sew the last round of the body to the underside of the head, and the arms to the sides of the body. Press the last round of each leg together, and sew to the side of the body using whip stitch. Sew the last round of the tail to the back of the body using whip stitch.

Percy
THE
PLATYPUS

Percy is the coolest platypus in town. That's because he is the most amazing colour. All his friends are as jealous as can be of his good looks.

HEIGHT
★ Approx. 17⅓in (44cm)

MATERIALS
★ Austermann Merino 160 (100% merino wool); 2 balls of Brombeer 220, 1 ball each of Honey 243 and Rosa 211, and scraps of Black 202 and White 201; 50g/174yd/160m
★ 2.5mm (B-1/UK 13) crochet hook
★ Toy stuffing
★ Tapestry needle

BODY

Work in rounds. At the end of each round, work 1 sl st into first st in round, 1 ch and turn.

Round 1: using Brombeer yarn, work 9 ch, 1 sc (UK dc) into second ch from hook, 1 sc (UK dc) into each of next 6 ch, 3 sc (UK dc) into last ch. Continue working on the other side of the length of ch: 6 sc (UK dc), 2 sc (UK dc) into same ch as first st (18 sts).

Round 2: inc 1 st, 6 sc (UK dc), inc 1 st three times, 6 sc (UK dc), inc 1 st twice (24 sts).

Round 3: 1 sc (UK dc), inc 1 st, 7 sc (UK dc), inc 1 st, 1 sc (UK dc), inc 1 st, 1 sc (UK dc), inc 1 st, 7 sc (UK dc), inc 1 st, 1 sc (UK dc), inc 1 st (30 sts).

Round 4: 2 sc (UK dc), inc 1 st, 8 sc (UK dc), inc 1 st, 2 sc (UK dc), inc 1 st, 2 sc (UK dc), inc 1 st, 8 sc (UK dc), inc 1 st, 2 sc (UK dc), inc 1 st (36 sts).

Round 5: 3 sc (UK dc), inc 1 st, 9 sc (UK dc), inc 1 st, 3 sc (UK dc), inc 1 st, 3 sc (UK dc), inc 1 st, 9 sc (UK dc), inc 1 st, 3 sc (UK dc), inc 1 st (42 sts).

Rounds 6 and 7: 1 sc (UK dc) into each st of previous round (42 sts).

Round 8: 4 sc (UK dc), inc 1 st, 10 sc (UK dc), inc 1 st, 4 sc (UK dc), inc 1 st, 4 sc (UK dc), inc 1 st, 10 sc (UK dc), inc 1 st, 4 sc (UK dc), inc 1 st (48 sts).

Round 9: 1 sc (UK dc) into each st of previous round (48 sts).

Round 10: *7 sc (UK dc), inc 1 st*, rep from * to * five more times (54 sts).

Rounds 11–26: 1 sc (UK dc) into each st of previous round (54 sts).

Round 27: *7 sc (UK dc), dec 1 st*, rep from * to * five more times (48 sts).

Round 28: *6 sc (UK dc), dec 1 st*, rep from * to * five more times (42 sts).

Round 29: *5 sc (UK dc), dec 1 st*, rep from * to * five more times (36 sts).

Round 30: 1 sc (UK dc) into each st of previous round (36 sts).

Round 31: *2 sc (UK dc), inc 1 st*, rep from * to * eleven more times (48 sts).

Rounds 32–37: 1 sc (UK dc) into each st of previous round (48 sts).

Round 38: *7 sc (UK dc), inc 1 st*, rep from * to * five more times (54 sts).

Rounds 39–48: 1 sc (UK dc) into each st of previous round (54 sts).

Round 49: *8 sc (UK dc), inc 1 st*, rep from * to * five more times (60 sts).

Rounds 50–53: 1 sc (UK dc) into each st of previous round (60 sts).

Round 54: *9 sc (UK dc), inc 1 st* rep from * to * five more times (66 sts).

Round 55: 1 sc (UK dc) into each st of previous round (66 sts).

Round 56: *10 sc (UK dc), inc 1 st* rep from * to * five more times (72 sts).

Round 57: *11 sc (UK dc), inc 1 st* rep from * to * five more times (78 sts).

Rounds 58–68: 1 sc (UK dc) into each st of previous round (78 sts).

Round 69: *11 sc (UK dc), dec 1 st*, rep from * to * five more times (72 sts).

Round 70: *10 sc (UK dc), dec 1 st*, rep from * to * five more times (66 sts).

Round 71: *9 sc (UK dc), dec 1 st*, rep from * to * five more times (60 sts).

Stuff the body.

Round 72: *8 sc (UK dc), dec 1 st*, rep from * to * five more times (54 sts).

Round 73: *7 sc (UK dc), dec 1 st*, rep from * to * five more times (48 sts).

Round 74: *6 sc (UK dc), dec 1 st*, rep from * to * five more times (42 sts).

Round 75: *5 sc (UK dc), dec 1 st*, rep from * to * five more times (36 sts).

Round 76: *4 sc (UK dc), dec 1 st*, rep from * to * five more times (30 sts).

Round 77: *3 sc (UK dc), dec 1 st*, rep from * to * five more times (24 sts).

Add a little more stuffing.

Round 78: *2 sc (UK dc), dec 1 st*, rep from * to * five more times (18 sts).

Round 79: *1 sc (UK dc), dec 1 st*, rep from * to * five more times (12 sts).

Round 80: dec 1 st six times (6 sts).

Round 81: *skip 1 st, 1 sl st*, rep from * to * twice more (3 sts).

Secure the yarn and fasten off.

BEAK

Work in rounds. At the end of each round, work 1 sl st into first st in round, 1 ch and turn.

Round 1: using Honey yarn, work 7 ch, 1 sc (UK dc) into second ch from hook, 1 sc (UK dc) into next 4 ch, 3 sc (UK dc) into the last ch. Continue working on the other side of the length of ch: 4 sc (UK dc), 2 sc (UK dc) into the same ch as the first st (14 sts).

Round 2: inc 1 st, 4 sc (UK dc), inc 1 st three times, 4 sc (UK dc), inc 1 st twice (20 sts).

Rounds 3–6: 1 sc (UK dc) into each st of previous round (20 sts).

Round 7: *9 sc (UK dc), inc 1 st*, rep from * to * once more (22 sts).

Round 8: 1 sc (UK dc) into each st of previous round (22 sts).

Round 9: *10 sc (UK dc), inc 1 st*, rep from * to * once more (24 sts).

Rounds 10 and 11: 1 sc (UK dc) into each st of previous round (24 sts).

Round 12: *11 sc (UK dc), inc 1 st*, rep from * to * once more (26 sts).

Rounds 13 and 14: 1 sc (UK dc) into each st of previous round (26 sts).

Round 15: 5 sc (UK dc), 1 hdc (UK htr), 2 dc (UK tr) in 1 st twice, 1 hdc (UK htr), 17 sc (UK dc) (28 sts).

Round 16: 6 sc (UK dc), inc 1 st, 2 sc (UK dc), inc 1 st, 18 sc (UK dc) (30 sts).

Round 17: 1 sc (UK dc), inc 1 st, 4 sc (UK dc), inc 1 st, 4 sc (UK dc), inc 1 st, 1 sc (UK dc), inc 1 st, 10 sc (UK dc), inc 1 sc (UK dc) (35 sts).

Secure yarn and fasten off, leaving a long tail. Stuff the beak.

BACK LEGS (MAKE 2)

Work in rounds. At the end of each round, work 1 sl st into first st in round, 1 ch and turn.

Round 1: using Honey yarn, work 6 sc (UK dc) into a magic ring (6 sts).

Round 2: *1 sc (UK dc), inc 1 st*, rep from * to * twice more (9 sts).

Rounds 3–5: 1 sc (UK dc) into each st of previous round (9 sts).

Secure the yarn and fasten off. Repeat rounds 1–5 twice more. Do not fasten off yarn at third toe (called "first toe" below), but continue working as follows:

Round 6: 3 sc (UK dc), 3 sc (UK dc) in second toe, 9 sc (UK dc) in last toe, 6 sc (UK dc) in remaining st of second toe, 6 sc (UK dc) in remaining st of first toe (27 sts).

Rounds 7–11: 1 sc (UK dc) into each st of previous round (27 sts).

Round 12: *7 sc (UK dc), dec 1 st*, rep from * to * twice more (24 sts).

Round 13: 1 sc (UK dc) into each st of previous round (24 sts).

Round 14: *2 sc (UK dc), dec 1 st*, rep from * to * five more times (18 sts).

Round 15: *1 sc (UK dc), dec 1 st*, rep from * to * five more times (12 sts).

Change to Brombeer yarn.

Round 16: 1 sc (UK dc) into each st of previous round (12 sts).

Round 17: *1 sc (UK dc), inc 1 st*, rep from * to * five more times (18 sts).

Rounds 18 and 19: 1 sc (UK dc) into each st of previous round (18 sts).

Round 20: *2 sc (UK dc), inc 1 st*, rep from * to * five more times (24 sts).

Round 21: 1 sc (UK dc) into each st of previous round (24 sts).

Round 22: *3 sc (UK dc), inc 1 st*, rep from * to * five more times (30 sts).

Rounds 23–26: 1 sc (UK dc) into each st of previous round (30 sts).

Secure the yarn and fasten off. Stuff the back leg to round 22.

FRONT LEGS (MAKE 2)

Work as back leg to round 19. Work round 20 as follows: 1 sc (UK dc) into each st of previous round. Secure yarn and fasten off. Stuff front leg to round 18.

EYES (MAKE 2)

Round 1: using Black yarn, work 6 sc (UK dc) into a magic ring (6 sts).

Join in a round with 1 sl st into the first st. Secure the yarn and fasten off.

TAIL

Work in rounds. At the end of each round, work 1 sl st into first st in round, 1 ch and turn.

Round 1: using Rosa yarn, work 6 sc (UK dc) into a magic ring (6 sts).

Round 2: inc 1 st six times (12 sts).

Round 3: 1 sc (UK dc) into each st of previous round (12 sts).

Round 4: 2 sc (UK dc), inc 1 st, 5 sc (UK dc), inc 1 st, 3 sc (UK dc) (14 sts).

Round 5: 1 sc (UK dc) into each st of previous round (14 sts).

Round 6: 3 sc (UK dc), inc 1 st, 6 sc (UK dc), inc 1 st, 3 sc (UK dc) (16 sts).

Round 7: 4 sc (UK dc), inc 1 st, 7 sc (UK dc), inc 1 st, 3 sc (UK dc) (18 sts).

Round 8: 5 sc (UK dc), inc 1 st, 8 sc (UK dc), inc 1 st, 3 sc (UK dc) (20 sts).

Round 9: 6 sc (UK dc), inc 1 st, 9 sc (UK dc), inc 1 st, 3 sc (UK dc) (22 sts).

Round 10: 7 sc (UK dc), inc 1 st, 10 sc (UK dc), inc 1 st, 3 sc (UK dc) (24 sts).

Round 11: 8 sc (UK dc), inc 1 st, 11 sc (UK dc), inc 1 st, 3 sc (UK dc) (26 sts).

Round 12: 9 sc (UK dc), inc 1 st, 12 sc (UK dc), inc 1 st, 3 sc (UK dc) (28 sts).

Round 13: 10 sc (UK dc), inc 1 st, 13 sc (UK dc), inc 1 st, 3 sc (UK dc) (30 sts).

Round 14: 11 sc (UK dc), inc 1 st, 14 sc (UK dc), inc 1 st, 3 sc (UK dc) (32 sts).

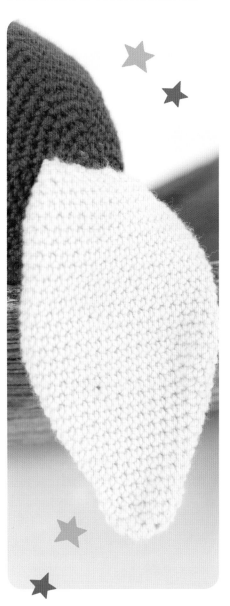

Round 15: 12 sc (UK dc), inc 1 st, 15 sc (UK dc), inc 1 st, 3 sc (UK dc) (34 sts).

Round 16: 13 sc (UK dc), inc 1 st, 16 sc (UK dc), inc 1 st, 3 sc (UK dc) (36 sts).

Rounds 17–29: 1 sc (UK dc) into each st of previous round (36 sts).

Round 30: 13 sc (UK dc), dec 1 st, 16 sc (UK dc), dec 1 st, 3 sc (UK dc) (34 sts).

Round 31: 12 sc (UK dc), dec 1 st, 15 sc (UK dc), dec 1 st, 3 sc (UK dc) (32 sts).

Round 32: 11 sc (UK dc), dec 1 st, 14 sc (UK dc), dec 1 st, 3 sc (UK dc) (30 sts).

Round 33: *3 sc (UK dc), dec 1 st*, rep from * to * five more times (24 sts).

Round 34: *2 sc (UK dc), dec 1 st*, rep from * to * five more times (18 sts).

Secure the yarn and fasten off. Do not stuff the tail.

FINISHING OFF

Sew the last round of the beak to the first round of the body using whip stitch. The dc (UK tr) of round 15 will be in the middle of the top of the beak. Sew the eyes to the sides of the body above the beak. Using White yarn, embroider two French knots to the eyes. Sew two eyelashes in Black yarn beside each eye. Press the last round of the front legs together, and sew to rounds 35–41 of the body using whip stitch. Press the last round of the back legs together, and sew to rounds 57–70 of the body using whip stitch. Press the last round of the tail together, and sew to the back of the platypus using whip stitch.

SOUTH AMERICA

Paul
THE SLOTH

Life is wonderful! Imagine hanging around all day in the sun, not having to do anything. That's Paul's favourite occupation. But from time to time, even he gets bored, and that's when he starts playing his guitar and singing along.

HEIGHT
* Approx. 17¹/₃in (44cm)

MATERIALS
* Lang Yarns Merino 70 (98% merino wool, 2% polyester); 4 balls of Pa-Bianco Cognac 0015 and 1 ball Mélange Beige 0022; 50g/76yd/70m
* Lang Yarns Merino 120 (100% merino wool); scraps of Dark Brown Mélange 0368 and Dark Beige Mélange 0326; 50g/131yd/120m
* Austermann Merino 160 (100% merino wool); scraps of Black 202 and White 201; 50g/174yd/160m
* 4mm (G-6/UK 8) and 2.5mm (B-1/UK 13) crochet hooks
* Toy stuffing
* Tapestry needle

BODY
The sloth is worked in one piece from the legs to the head. Start with the legs. Work in spiral rounds. This means the rounds are not finished with a sl st, nor do you work a turning ch at the beg of a new round.

Round 1: using 4mm (G-6/UK 8) hook and Pa-Bianco Cognac yarn, work 6 sc (UK dc) into a magic ring (6 sts).

Round 2: inc 1 st six times (12 sts).

Round 3: *1 sc (UK dc), inc 1 st*, rep from * to * five more times (18 sts).

Round 4: *2 sc (UK dc), inc 1 st*, rep from * to * five more times (24 sts).

Rounds 5–20: 1 sc (UK dc) into each st of previous round (24 sts).

Round 21: inc 1 st twice, 22 sc (UK dc) (26 sts).

Round 22: inc 1 st, 2 sc (UK dc), inc 1 st, 22 sc (UK dc) (28 sts).

Round 23: inc 1 st, 4 sc (UK dc), inc 1 st, 22 sc (UK dc) (30 sts).

Secure the yarn and fasten off. Repeat rounds 1–20 for the other leg. Continue as follows:

Round 21: 2 sc (UK dc), inc 1 st twice, 20 sc (UK dc) (26 sts).

Round 22: 2 sc (UK dc), inc 1 st, 2 sc (UK dc), inc 1 st, 20 sc (UK dc) (28 sts).

Round 23: 2 sc (UK dc), inc 1 st, 4 sc (UK dc), inc 1 st, 20 sc (UK dc) (30 sts).

Do not fasten off the yarn, but continue working the two legs together as follows:

Round 24: 6 sc (UK dc), continue working at 5th st of first leg: 30 sc (UK dc), continue working at 7th st of second leg: 24 sc (UK dc) (60 sts).

Rounds 25–36: 1 sc (UK dc) into each st of previous round (60 sts).

Stuff the legs.

Round 37: *8 sc (UK dc), dec 1 st*, rep from * to * five more times (54 sts).

Rounds 38 and 39: 1 sc (UK dc) into each st of previous round (54 sts).

Round 40: *7 sc (UK dc), dec 1 st*, rep from * to * five more times (48 sts).

Rounds 41–50: 1 sc (UK dc) into each st of previous round (48 sts).

Stuff the body.

Round 51: *6 sc (UK dc), dec 1 st*, rep from * to * five more times (42 sts).

Round 52: *5 sc (UK dc), dec 1 st*, rep from * to * five more times (36 sts).

Rounds 53 and 54: 1 sc (UK dc) into each st of previous round (36 sts).

Round 55: *5 sc (UK dc), inc 1 st*, rep from * to * five more times (42 sts).

Rounds 56–67: 1 sc (UK dc) into each st of previous round (42 sts).

Round 68: *5 sc (UK dc), dec 1 st*, rep from * to * five more times (36 sts).

Round 69: *4 sc (UK dc), dec 1 st*, rep from * to * five more times (30 sts).

Stuff the head.

Round 70: *3 sc (UK dc), dec 1 st*, rep from * to * five more times (24 sts).

Round 71: *2 sc (UK dc), dec 1 st*, rep from * to * five more times (18 sts).

Round 72: *1 sc (UK dc), dec 1 st*, rep from * to * five more times (12 sts).

Round 73: dec 1 st six times (6 st).

Round 74: *skip 1 st, 1 sl st*, rep from * to * twice more (3 sts).

Secure the yarn and fasten off.

FEET (MAKE 2)
Work in spiral rounds. This means the rounds are not finished with a sl st, nor do you work a turning ch at the beg of a new round.

Round 1: using 4mm (G-6/UK 8) hook and Mélange Beige yarn, work 6 sc (UK dc) into a magic ring (6 sts).

Round 2: 1 sc (UK dc) into each st of previous round (6 sts).

Round 3: *1 sc (UK dc), inc 1 st*, rep from * to * twice more (9 sts).

Round 4: *2 sc (UK dc), inc 1 st*, rep from * to * twice more (12 sts).

Round 5: 1 sc (UK dc) into each st of previous round (12 sts).

Round 6: *3 sc (UK dc), inc 1 st*, rep from * to * twice more (15 sts).

Rounds 7–11: 1 sc (UK dc) into each st of previous round (15 sts).

Secure yarn and fasten off. Stuff the foot lightly.

ARMS (MAKE 2)

Work in spiral rounds. This means the rounds are not finished with a sl st, nor do you work a turning ch at the beg of a new round.

Round 1: using 4mm (G-6/UK 8) hook and Pa-Bianco Cognac yarn, work 6 sc (UK dc) into a magic ring (6 sts).

Round 2: inc 1 st six times (12 sts).

Round 3: *1 sc (UK dc), inc 1 st*, rep from * to * five more times (18 sts).

Rounds 4-31: 1 sc (UK dc) into each st of previous round (18 sts).

Round 32: *4 sc (UK dc), dec 1 st*, rep from * to * twice more (15 sts).

Rounds 33 and 34: 1 sc (UK dc) into each st of previous round (15 sts).

Round 35: *3 sc (UK dc), dec 1 st*, rep from * to * twice more (12 sts).

Rounds 36 and 37: 1 sc (UK dc) into each st of previous round (12 sts).

Secure the yarn and fasten off. Lightly stuff the arm three-quarters full.

FACE

Work in spiral rounds. This means the rounds are not finished with a sl st, nor do you work a turning ch at the beg of a new round.

Round 1: using 4mm (G-6/UK 8) hook and Dark Beige Mélange yarn, work 6 sc (UK dc) into a magic ring (6 sts).

Round 2: inc 1 st six times (12 sts).

Round 3: *1 sc (UK dc), inc 1 st*, rep from * to * five more times (18 sts).

Round 4: *2 sc (UK dc), inc 1 st*, rep from * to * five more times (24 sts).

Round 5: 3 sc (UK dc), 3 hdc (UK htr) in 1 st, 1 dc (UK tr), 2 dc (UK tr) in 1 st, 1 sc (UK dc), 2 ch, 1 sc (UK dc), 2 dc (UK tr) in 1 st, 1 dc (UK tr), 3 hdc (UK htr) in 1 st, 2 sc (UK dc), 2 sc (UK dc) in 1 st, 2 sc (UK dc), 1 sl st.

Secure the yarn and fasten off.

NOSE

Round 1: using 2.5mm (B-1/UK 13) hook and Dark Brown Mélange yarn, work 8 sc (UK dc) into a magic ring (8 sts).

Secure the yarn and fasten off.

MOUTH

Round 1: using 2.5mm (B-1/UK 13) hook and Mélange Beige yarn, work 8 sc (UK dc) into a magic ring (8 sts).

Round 2: 1 sc (UK dc), [1 hdc (UK htr), 1 dc (UK tr), 1 ch, 1 dc (UK tr), 1 hdc (UK htr)] in 1 st, 1 sc (UK dc), 3 sc (UK dc) in 1 st, 1 sc (UK dc), [1 hdc (UK htr), 1 dc (UK tr), 1 ch, 1 dc (UK tr), 1 hdc (UK htr)] in 1 st, 1 sc (UK dc), 3 sc (UK dc) in 1 st.

Secure the yarn and fasten off.

EYE SPOTS (MAKE 2)

Round 1: using 2.5mm (B-1/UK 13) hook and Dark Brown Mélange yarn, work 8 ch, 1 sl st into second ch from hook, 1 sc (UK dc), 3 hdc (UK htr), 1 dc (UK tr), 6 dc (UK tr) into last ch. Continue working on the other side of the length of ch: 1 hdc (UK htr), 2 sc (UK dc), 3 ch, skip 1 sc (UK dc), 1 sl st into first st of the round.

Secure the yarn and fasten off.

EYES (MAKE 2)

Round 1: using 2.5mm (B-1/UK 13) hook and Black yarn work 6 sc (UK dc) into a magic ring (6 sts).

Join with 1 sl st in first st to make a ring. Secure the yarn and fasten off.

FINISHING OFF

Press the last round of each arm together, and sew the edge to the sides of the body at round 52 using whip stitch. Sew up the little opening between the legs with mattress stitch. Use backstitch to sew the face to the front of the head. Make sure that the 2 ch of round 5 of the face are on top. Sew the eye spots along the edge of the face with backstitch. Sew the mouth to the face in the same way, and then the nose to the upper part of the mouth. Sew an eye to each eye spot. Using White yarn, embroider two French knots to each eye. Then sew two semi-circles in White yarn around the eyes. For the lips, sew a horizontal stitch with Black yarn, and secure in the middle with a small stitch. Sew the last round of a foot to the first round of each leg.

Emilio
THE CHAMELEON

Emilio is a real charmer. He can delight any lady chameleon in moments with his colour changes. They always like it when he chooses their favourite colour. But Emilio's favourite colour is definitely yellow.

LENGTH
★ Approx. 13in (33cm)

MATERIALS
★ Lang Yarns Merino+ Color (100% merino wool); 1 ball of Green/Yellow 0011; 100g/196yd/180m
★ Austermann Merino 160 (100% merino wool); scraps of Black 202 and White 201; 50g/174yd/160m
★ 3mm (D-3/UK 11) and 2.5mm (B-1/UK 13) crochet hooks
★ Toy stuffing
★ Tapestry needle

BODY
The chameleon is worked in one piece from head to tail. Start at the head. Work in rounds. At the end of each round, work 1 sl st into first st in round, 1 ch and turn.

Round 1: using 3mm (D-3/UK 11) hook and Green/Yellow yarn, work 6 sc (UK dc) into a magic ring (6 sts).

Round 2: inc 1 st six times (12 sts).

Round 3: *1 sc (UK dc), inc 1 st*, rep from * to * five more times (18 sts).

Round 4: 1 sc (UK dc) into each st of previous round (18 sts).

Round 5: *1 sc (UK dc), inc 1 st*, rep from * to * eight more times (27 sts).

Round 6: *2 sc (UK dc), inc 1 st*, rep from * to * eight more times (27 sts).

Round 7: *3 sc (UK dc), inc 1 st*, rep from * to * eight more times (45 sts).

Rounds 8–14: 1 sc (UK dc) into each st of previous round (45 sts).

Round 15: 20 sc (UK dc), inc 1 st, 1 sc (UK dc), inc 1 st, 1 sc (UK dc), inc 1 st, 20 sc (UK dc) (48 sts).

Rounds 16–19: 1 sc (UK dc) into each st of previous round (48 sts).

Round 20: 1 raised sc (UK dc) around the back in each st of previous round (48 sts).

Rounds 21 and 22: 1 sc (UK dc) into each st of previous round (48 sts).

Round 23: 20 sc (UK dc), dec 1 st, 2 sc (UK dc), dec 1 st, 2 sc (UK dc), dec 1 st, 18 sc (UK dc) (45 sts).

Round 24–27: 1 sc (UK dc) into each st of previous round (45 sts).

Round 28: 18 sc (UK dc), dec 1 st, 4 sc (UK dc), dec 1 st, 4 sc (UK dc), dec 1 st, 13 sc (UK dc) (42 sts).

Rounds 29–37: 1 sc (UK dc) into each st of previous round (42 sts).

Round 38: 19 sc (UK dc), dec 1 st, 3 sc (UK dc), dec 1 st, 3 sc (UK dc), dec 1 st, 11 sc (UK dc) (39 sts).

Rounds 39 and 40: 1 sc (UK dc) into each st of previous round (39 sts).

Round 41: 17 sc (UK dc), dec 1 st, 4 sc (UK dc), dec 1 st, 4 sc (UK dc), dec 1 st, 8 sc (UK dc) (36 sts).

Rounds 42 and 43: 1 sc (UK dc) into each st of previous round (36 sts).

Round 44: 3 sc (UK dc), inc 1 st, 1 sc (UK dc), inc 1 st, 14 sc (UK dc), dec 1 st, 2 sc (UK dc), dec 1 st, 10 sc (UK dc) (36 sts).

Round 45: 19 sc (UK dc), dec 1 st, 6 sc (UK dc), dec 1 st, 7 sc (UK dc) (34 sts).

Round 46: 17 sc (UK dc), dec 1 st, 8 sc (UK dc), dec 1 st, 5 sc (UK dc) (32 sts).

Round 47: 4 sc (UK dc), inc 1 st, 1 sc (UK dc), inc 1 st, 13 sc (UK dc), dec 1 st, 1 sc (UK dc), dec 1 st, 7 sc (UK dc) (32 sts).

Round 48: 18 sc (UK dc), dec 1 st, 7 sc (UK dc), dec 1 st, 3 sc (UK dc) (30 sts).

Round 49: 19 sc (UK dc), dec 1 st, 4 sc (UK dc), dec 1 st, 3 sc (UK dc) (28 sts).

Round 50: 5 sc (UK dc), inc 1 st, 3 sc (UK dc), inc 1 st, 8 sc (UK dc), dec 1 st, 4 sc (UK dc), dec 1 st, 2 sc (UK dc) (28 sts).

Round 51: 19 sc (UK dc), dec 1 st, 4 sc (UK dc), dec 1 st, 1 sc (UK dc) (26 sts).

Round 52: 18 sc (UK dc), dec 1 st, 4 sc (UK dc), dec 1 st (23 sts).

Round 53: dec 1 st, 14 sc (UK dc), dec 1 st, 2 sc (UK dc), dec 1 st, 2 sc (UK dc) (21 sts).

Rounds 54 and 55: 1 sc (UK dc) into each st of previous round (21 sts).

Round 56: 1 sc (UK dc), dec 1 st, 11 sc (UK dc), dec 1 st, 2 sc (UK dc), dec 1 st, 1 sc (UK dc) (18 sts).

Rounds 57 and 58: 1 sc (UK dc) into each st of previous round (18 sts).

Round 59: dec 1 st, 12 sc (UK dc), dec 1 st twice (15 sts).

Round 60: 1 sc (UK dc) into each st of previous round (15 sts).

Rounds 61–63: dec 1 st, 5 sc (UK dc), inc 1 st twice, 4 sc (UK dc), dec 1 st (15 sts).

Round 64: dec 1 st, 11 sc (UK dc), dec 1 st (13 sts).

Round 65: dec 1 st, 5 sc (UK dc), inc 1 st, 3 sc (UK dc), dec 1 st (12 sts).

Round 66: dec 1 st, 4 sc (UK dc), inc 1 st, 3 sc (UK dc), dec 1 st (11 sts).

Round 67: dec 1 st, 3 sc (UK dc), inc 1 st, 3 sc (UK dc), dec 1 st (10 sts).

Rounds 68–76: dec 1 st, 2 sc (UK dc), inc 1 st twice, 2 sc (UK dc), dec 1 st (10 sts).

Round 77: dec 1 st, 6 sc (UK dc), dec 1 st (8 sts).

Rounds 78–91: dec 1 st, 1 sc (UK dc), inc 1 st twice, 1 sc (UK dc), dec 1 st (8 sts).

Round 92: dec 1 st, 4 sc (UK dc), dec 1 st (6 sts).

Round 93: dec 1 st, 2 sc (UK dc), dec 1 st (4 sts).

Round 94: dec 1 st twice (2 sts).

Secure the yarn and fasten off.

FRONT LEGS (MAKE 2)

Work in spiral rounds. This means the rounds are not finished with a sl st, nor do you work a turning ch at the beg of a new round.

Round 1: using 3mm (D-3/UK 11) hook and Green/Yellow yarn, work 6 sc (UK dc) into a magic ring (6 sts).

Rounds 2–14: 1 sc (UK dc) into each st of previous round (6 sts).

Round 15: inc 1 st twice, 4 sc (UK dc) (8 sts).

Round 16: inc 1 st four times, 4 sc (UK dc) (12 sts).

Rounds 17 and 18: 1 sc (UK dc) into each st of previous round (12 sts).

Round 19: work into the back bar of the stitch only: dec 1 st six times (6 sts).

Round 20: *skip 1 st, 1 sl st*, rep from * to * twice more (3 sts).

Secure the yarn and fasten off.

BACK LEGS (MAKE 2)

Work in spiral rounds. The rounds are not closed with 1 sl st, nor do you work a turning ch at the beg of a new round.

Round 1: using 3mm (D-3/UK 11) hook and Green/Yellow yarn, work 6 sc (UK dc) into a magic ring (6 sts).

Rounds 2–9: 1 sc (UK dc) into each st of previous round (6 sts).

Work rounds 10–15 following the instructions for rounds 15–20 of the Front Legs. Secure yarn and fasten off.

EYES (MAKE 2)

Round 1: using 2.5mm (B-1/UK 13) hook and Green/Yellow yarn, work 13 dc (UK tr) into a magic ring. Join in a round with 1 sl st into the first st. Secure yarn and fasten off.

PUPIL

Round 1: using 2.5mm (B-1/UK 13) hook and Black yarn, work 6 sc (UK dc) into a magic ring (6 sts).

Join in a round with 1 sl st into the first st. Secure the yarn and fasten off.

COMB

Work in rows. Work 1 ch at the end of the row and turn the work.

Join Green/Yellow yarn to the middle of round 20 of the body (the round of raised sc (UK dc), and work along the top of the chameleon's head towards the nose:

Row 1: 1 sl st, 1 sc (UK dc), 1 hdc (UK htr), 6 dc (UK tr), 1 hdc (UK htr), 1 sc (UK dc), 1 sl st (12 sts).

Row 2: 1 sl st, 1 sc (UK dc), 1 hdc (UK htr), 2 dc (UK tr) in 1 st, 4 dc (UK tr), 1 hdc (UK htr), 1 sc (UK dc), 2 sl st (13 sts).

Secure the yarn and fasten off.

FINISHING OFF

Sew the eyes to rounds 11–16 of the head on the sides so that the comb is right between them. Then sew a pupil to each eye. Using White yarn, embroider two French knots to each pupil, then two semi-circles around the eyes.

Sew the first round of each front leg to rounds 24 and 25 of the body using whip stitch. Bend the leg in the middle so it arches towards the tail, and secure to the body with a few stitches. Sew the back legs to rounds 43 and 44 of the body in the same way, with the bend pointing towards the head. Turn the last rounds of the body into a tail, by pressing them together and lightly coiling them. Secure to the body and within the tail with a few stitches.

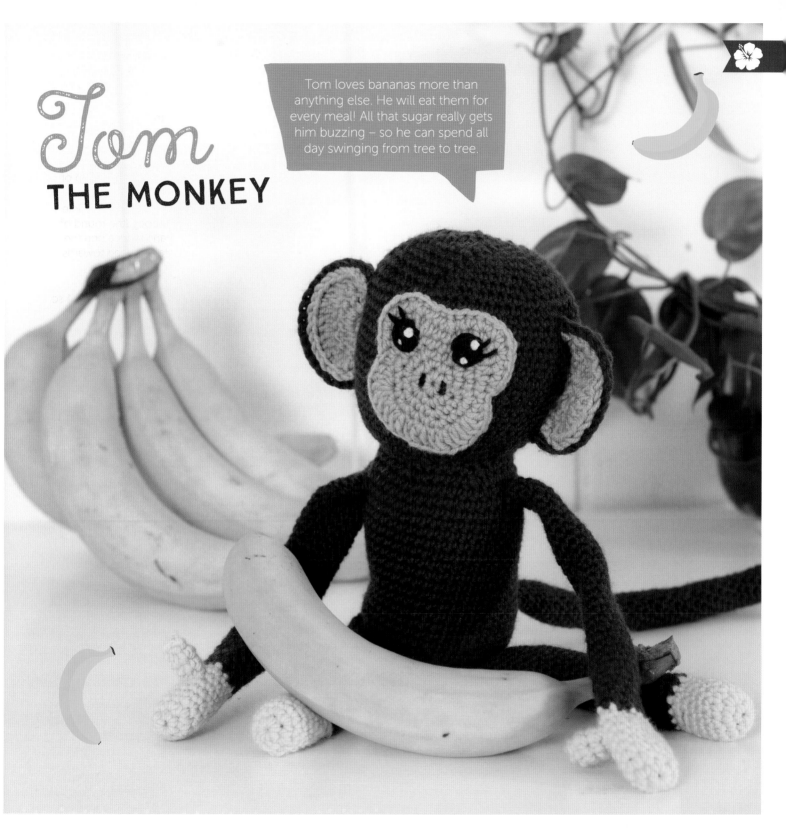

Tom
THE MONKEY

Tom loves bananas more than anything else. He will eat them for every meal! All that sugar really gets him buzzing – so he can spend all day swinging from tree to tree.

HEIGHT

★ Approx. 13in (33cm)

MATERIALS

★ Lana Grossa Cool Wool Big (100% wool); 2 balls of Brown 644; 50g/131yd/120m
★ Lang Yarns Merino 120 (100% merino wool); small amounts of Gold 0149 and Pink 0019; 50g/131yd/120m
★ Austermann Merino 160 (100% merino wool); scraps of Black 202 and White 201; 50g/174yd/160m
★ 2.5mm (B-1/UK 13) crochet hook
★ Toy stuffing
★ Tapestry needle

BODY

Work in spiral rounds. This means the rounds are not finished with a sl st, nor do you work a turning ch at the beg of a new round.

Round 1: using Brown yarn, work 6 sc (UK dc) into a magic ring (6 sts).

Round 2: inc 1 st six times (12 sts).

Round 3: *1 sc (UK dc), inc 1 st*, rep from * to * five more times (18 sts).

Round 4: *2 sc (UK dc), inc 1 st*, rep from * to * five more times (24 sts).

Round 5: *3 sc (UK dc), inc 1 st*, rep from * to * five more times (30 sts).

Round 6: *4 sc (UK dc), inc 1 st*, rep from * to * five more times (36 sts).

Round 7: *5 sc (UK dc), inc 1 st*, rep from * to * five more times (42 sts).

Rounds 8–25: 1 sc (UK dc) into each st of previous round (42 sts).

Round 26: *5 sc (UK dc), dec 1 st*, rep from * to * five more times (36 sts).

Round 27: *4 sc (UK dc), dec 1 st*, rep from * to * five more times (30 sts).

Round 28: *3 sc (UK dc), dec 1 st*, rep from * to * five more times (24 sts).

The body now transitions to the head.

Round 29: inc 1 st twenty-four times (48 sts).

Round 30: *7 sc (UK dc), inc 1 st*, rep from * to * five more times (54 sts).

Round 31: *8 sc (UK dc), inc 1 st*, rep from * to * five more times (60 sts).

Rounds 32–46: 1 sc (UK dc) into each st of previous round (60 sts).

Round 47: *8 sc (UK dc), dec 1 st*, rep from * to * five more times (54 sts).

Round 48: *7 sc (UK dc), dec 1 st*, rep from * to * five more times (48 sts).

Stuff the body and head.

Round 49: *6 sc (UK dc), dec 1 st*, rep from * to * five more times (42 sts).

Round 50: *5 sc (UK dc), dec 1 st*, rep from * to * five more times (36 sts).

Round 51: *4 sc (UK dc), dec 1 st*, rep from * to * five more times (30 sts).

Round 52: *3 sc (UK dc), dec 1 st*, rep from * to * five more times (24 sts).

Round 53: *2 sc (UK dc), dec 1 st*, rep from * to * five more times (18 sts).

Round 54: *1 sc (UK dc), dec 1 st*, rep from * to * five more times (12 sts).

Round 55: dec 1 st six times (6 sts).

Round 56: *skip 1 st, 1 sl st*, rep from * to * twice more (3 sts).

Secure the yarn and fasten off.

ARMS (MAKE 2)

Work in spiral rounds. This means the rounds are not finished with a sl st, nor do you work a turning ch at the beg of a new round. Place marker at beg of round to make it easier to find.

Round 1: using Gold yarn, work 6 sc (UK dc) into a magic ring (6 sts).

Round 2: inc 1 st six times (12 sts).

Rounds 3–7: 1 sc (UK dc) into each st of previous round (12 sts).

Round 8: 2 sc (UK dc), 2 ch, skip 2 st, 8 sc (UK dc) (12 sts).

Round 9: 1 sc (UK dc) into each st of previous round (12 sts).

Change to Brown yarn.

Rounds 10–40: 1 sc (UK dc) into each st of previous round (12 sts).

Secure the yarn and fasten off. Do not stuff the arms.

THUMBS

Join Gold yarn to the first working st in round 8 of arm, and work 1 round of 6 sc (UK dc) into the opening. Join in a round with 1 sl st into the first st.

Rounds 2–3: 1 sc (UK dc) into each st of previous round (6 sts).

Secure the yarn and fasten off. Repeat for the second arm.

LEGS (MAKE 2)

Work in spiral rounds. This means the rounds are not finished with a sl st, nor do you work a turning ch at the beg of a new round. Place marker at beg of round to make it easier to find.

Round 1: using Gold yarn, work 6 sc (UK dc) into a magic ring (6 sts).

Round 2: inc 1 st six times (12 sts).

Rounds 3–9: 1 sc (UK dc) into each st of previous round (12 sts).

Change to Brown yarn.

Rounds 10–34: 1 sc (UK dc) into each st of previous round (12 sts).

Secure the yarn and fasten off. Loosely stuff the legs.

EARS (MAKE 2 BROWN AND 2 PINK)

Work in rows. Start each row with 3 ch (count as first dc (UK tr)).

Row 1: work 6 dc (UK tr) into a magic ring (6 sts).

Row 2: 2 dc (UK tr) in 1 st six times (12 sts).

Row 3: *1 dc (UK tr), 2 dc (UK tr) in 1 st*, rep from * to * five more times (18 sts).

Secure the yarn and fasten off, leaving long yarn tails on the brown ears.

Place the wrong side of one pink ear against the wrong side of a brown ear and sew along the rounded edge in backstitch to join the two halves together. Hold the ear with the brown half facing you and the rounded edge facing away from you. Join Brown yarn to the first st of the last row of the brown half, and work 1 sc (UK dc) into each st of the third row.

FACE

Work in rounds. At the end of each round, work 1 sl st into first st in round, 1 ch and turn.

Round 1: using Pink yarn, work 6 sc (UK dc) into a magic ring (6 sts).

Round 2: inc 1 st six times (12 sts).

Round 3: *1 sc (UK dc), inc 1 st*, rep from * to * five more times (18 sts).

Round 4: *2 sc (UK dc), inc 1 st*, rep from * to * five more times (24 sts).

Round 5: 1 sc (UK dc), 1 hdc (UK htr), 5 dc (UK tr) in 1 st, 1 hdc (UK htr), 3 sc (UK dc), 1 hdc (UK htr), 5 dc (UK tr) in 1 st, 1 hdc (UK htr), 2 sc (UK dc), 1 hdc (UK htr), 3 dc (UK tr) in 1 st, 2 dc (UK tr) in 1 st twice, 1 dc (UK tr), 2 dc (UK tr) in 1 st twice, 1 dc (UK tr), 2 dc (UK tr) in 1 st twice, 3 dc (UK tr) in 1 st, 1 hdc (UK htr), 1 sc (UK dc) (41 sts).

Round 6: 3 sc (UK dc), inc 1 st three times, 2 sc (UK dc), dec 1 st, 3 sc (UK dc), inc 1 st three times, 2 sc (UK dc), [1 sc (UK dc) and 1 ch] in 1 st (24 sts). Do not work the remaining st.

Secure the yarn and fasten off.

EYES (MAKE 2)

Round 1: using Black yarn, work 6 sc (UK dc) into a magic ring (6 sts). Join in a round with 1 sl st into the first st.

Secure the yarn and fasten off.

TAIL

Work in spiral rounds. This means the rounds are not finished with a sl st, nor do you work a turning ch at the beg of a new round. Place marker at beg of round to make it easier to find.

Round 1: using Brown yarn, work 6 sc (UK dc) into a magic ring (6 sts).

Round 2: *1 sc (UK dc), inc 1 st*, rep from * to * twice more (9 sts).

Rounds 3–42: 1 sc (UK dc) into each st of previous round (9 sts).

Secure the yarn and fasten off. Loosely stuff the tail.

FINISHING OFF

Press the last round of each arm together, and use whip stitch to sew the edge to the side of the body at round 23. Make sure that the thumbs are pointing towards the middle of the body when you sew the arms on. Press the last round of each leg together, and use whip stitch to sew the edges to the sides of the body at round 6. Use whip stitch to sew the last round of the tail to the bottom of the back of the body. Use backstitch to sew the edge of the face to the front of the head. The dc (UK tr) from round 5 should be at the bottom. Sew the eyes to the face. Using White yarn, embroider two French knots onto the eyes. Using Black yarn, sew two small lines beside each eye for the eyelashes. Use whip stitch to sew the ears to the right and left of the face at rounds 33–45 of the head, with the pink side facing forward. Squeeze the ear a little so that the pink side is slightly rounded to the inside.

WATER

Henry
THE WHALE

He is at home in the Norwegian fjords: Henry the cuddly whale. Although he loves his home, he is often drawn out into the wide world. This means he is always finding new friends, and has also learnt several new languages. At the moment, he is practising his Japanese. "Konnichiwa!"

風

土

LENGTH
★ Approx. 13in (33cm)

MATERIALS
★ Lang Yarns Merino 70 (98% merino wool, 2% polyester); 2 balls of Pa-Bianco Mint 0058 and 1 ball of Bianco-Lachs 0027; 50g/76yd/70m
★ Austermann Merino 160 (100% merino wool); scraps of Black 202 and White 201; 50g/175yd/160m
★ 3mm (D-3/UK 11) and 2.5mm (B-1/UK 13) crochet hooks
★ Toy stuffing
★ Tapestry needle

TOP
Work in rows. Work 1 ch at the end of each row and turn the work.

Row 1: using 3mm (D-3/UK 11) hook and Pa-Bianco Mint yarn, work 3 sc (UK dc) into a magic ring (3 sts) (wrong side).

Row 2: inc 1 st three times (6 sts).

Row 3: *1 sc (UK dc), inc 1 st*, rep from * to * twice more (9 sts).

Row 4: *2 sc (UK dc), inc 1 st*, rep from * to * twice more (12 sts).

Row 5: *3 sc (UK dc), inc 1 st*, rep from * to * twice more (15 sts).

Row 6: *4 sc (UK dc), inc 1 st*, rep from * to * twice more (18 sts).

Row 7: *5 sc (UK dc), inc 1 st*, rep from * to * twice more (21 sts).

Row 8: *6 sc (UK dc), inc 1 st*, rep from * to * twice more (24 sts).

Row 9: 3 sc (UK dc), inc 1 st, *7 sc (UK dc), inc 1 st*, rep from * to * once more, 4 sc (UK dc) (27 sts).

Row 10: *8 sc (UK dc), inc 1 st*, rep from * to * twice more (30 sts).

Row 11: 4 sc (UK dc), inc 1 st, *9 sc (UK dc), inc 1 st*, rep from * to * once more, 5 sc (UK dc) (33 sts).

Row 12: *inc 1 st, 10 sc (UK dc)*, rep from * to * twice more (36 sts).

Row 13: 1 sc (UK dc) into each st of previous row (36 sts).

Row 14: 17 sc (UK dc), inc 1 st twice, 17 sc (UK dc) (38 sts).

Row 15: 1 sc (UK dc) into each st of previous row (38 sts).

Row 16: 18 sc (UK dc), inc 1 st twice, 18 sc (UK dc) (40 sts).

Row 17: 1 sc (UK dc) into each st of previous row (40 sts).

Row 18: 19 sc (UK dc), inc 1 st twice, 19 sc (UK dc) (42 sts).

Rows 19–36: 1 sc (UK dc) into each st of previous row (42 sts).

Row 37: *12 sc (UK dc), dec 1 st*, rep from * to * twice more (39 sts).

Row 38: 6 sc (UK dc), dec 1 st, *11 sc (UK dc), dec 1 st*, rep from * to * once more, 5 sc (UK dc) (36 sts).

Row 39: 2 sc (UK dc), dec 1 st, *10 sc (UK dc), dec 1 st*, rep from * to * once more, 8 sc (UK dc) (33 sts).

Row 40: 2 sc (UK dc), dec 1 st, *9 sc (UK dc), dec 1 st*, rep from * to * once more, 7 sc (UK dc) (30 sts).

Row 41: 2 sc (UK dc), dec 1 st, *8 sc (UK dc), dec 1 st*, rep from * to * once more, 6 sc (UK dc) (27 sts).

Row 42: *7 sc (UK dc), dec 1 st*, rep from * to * twice more (24 sts).

Rows 43 and 44: 1 sc (UK dc) into each st of previous row (24 sts).

Row 45: 10 sc (UK dc), dec 1 st twice, 10 sc (UK dc) (22 sts).

Row 46: 8 sc (UK dc), dec 1 st, 2 sc (UK dc), dec 1 st, 8 sc (UK dc) (20 sts).

Row 47: 4 sc (UK dc), dec 1 st, 8 sc (UK dc), dec 1 st, 4 sc (UK dc) (18 sts).

Row 48: *4 sc (UK dc), dec 1 st*, rep from * to * twice more (15 sts).

Rows 49–53: 1 sc (UK dc) into each st of previous row (15 sts).

Row 54: dec 1 st, 5 sc (UK dc), inc 1 st, 5 sc (UK dc), dec 1 st (14 sts).

Row 55: 1 sc (UK dc) into each st of previous row (14 sts).

Row 56: dec 1 st, 4 sc (UK dc), inc 1 st twice, 4 sc (UK dc), dec 1 st (14 sts).

Row 57: 1 sc (UK dc) into each st of previous row (14 sts).

Row 58: dec 1 st, 4 sc (UK dc), inc 1 st twice, 4 sc (UK dc), dec 1 st (14 sts).

Row 59: 14 sc (UK dc), 4 ch (18 sts). From here, always work 1 sl st in the first st of the row, 1 ch, and turn work.

Row 60: dec 1 st twice, 6 sc (UK dc), inc 1 st twice, 6 sc (UK dc) (18 sts).

Row 61: 1 sc (UK dc) into each st of previous row (18 sts).

Row 62: 1 sc (UK dc), dec 1 st, 6 sc (UK dc), inc 1 st twice, 5 sc (UK dc), dec 1 st (18 sts). Sl st into first st, do not turn.

Row 63: *1 sc (UK dc), dec 1 st*, rep from * to * five more times (12 sts).

Row 64: dec 1 st six times (6 sts).

Row 65: *skip 1 st, 1 sl st*, rep from * to * twice more (3 sts).

Secure the yarn and fasten off.

TUMMY
Work in rows. Work 1 ch at the end of each row and turn the work.

Row 1: using 3mm (D-3/UK 11) hook and Bianco-Lachs yarn, work 3 sc (UK dc) into a magic ring (3 sts).

Row 2: inc 1 st three times (6 sts).

Row 3: *1 sc (UK dc), inc 1 st*, rep from * to * twice more (9 sts).

Row 4: *2 sc (UK dc), inc 1 st*, rep from * to * twice more (12 sts).

Row 5: *3 sc (UK dc), inc 1 st*, rep from * to * twice more (15 sts).

Row 6: *4 sc (UK dc), inc 1 st*, rep from * to * twice more (18 sts).

Row 7: *5 sc (UK dc), inc 1 st*, rep from * to * twice more (21 sts).

Row 8: 3 sc (UK dc), inc 1 st, *6 sc (UK dc), inc 1 st*, rep from * to * once more, 3 sc (UK dc) (24 sts).

Row 9: *7 sc (UK dc), inc 1 st*, rep from * to * twice more (27 sts).

Row 10: 4 sc (UK dc), inc 1 st, *8 sc (UK dc), inc 1 st*, rep from * to * once more, 4 sc (UK dc) (30 sts).

Secure the yarn and fasten off. Join Bianco-Lachs yarn to end of row 10 and continue working in rows as follows:

Row 1: work 1 sc (UK dc) in the end of each row (20 sts).

Rows 2–21: 1 sc (UK dc) into each st of previous row (20 sts).

Row 22: dec 1 st, 16 sc (UK dc), dec 1 st (18 sts).

Row 23: dec 1 st, 14 sc (UK dc), dec 1 st (16 sts).

Row 24: dec 1 st, 12 sc (UK dc), dec 1 st (14 sts).

Rows 25–38: 1 sc (UK dc) into each st of previous row (14 sts).

Row 39: dec 1 st, 10 sc (UK dc), dec 1 st (12 sts).

Row 40: dec 1 st, 8 sc (UK dc), dec 1 st (10 sts).

Row 41: dec 1 st, 6 sc (UK dc), dec 1 st (8 sts).

Row 42: dec 1 st, 4 sc (UK dc), dec 1 st (6 sts).

Row 43: dec 1 st, 2 sc (UK dc), dec 1 st (4 sts).

Secure the yarn and fasten off.

TAIL LOBES (MAKE 2)

Work in rounds. At the end of each work 1 sl st into first st in round, 1 ch and turn.

Round 1: using 3mm (D-3/UK 11) hook and Pa-Bianco Mint yarn, work 6 sc (UK dc) into a magic ring (6 sts).

Round 2: 1 sc (UK dc) into each st of previous round (6 sts).

Round 3: 2 sc (UK dc), inc 1 st twice, 2 sc (UK dc) (8 sts).

Round 4: 1 sc (UK dc) into each st of previous round (8 sts).

Round 5: 3 sc (UK dc), inc 1 st twice, 3 sc (UK dc) (10 sts).

Round 6: 1 sc (UK dc) into each st of previous round (10 sts).

Round 7: 4 sc (UK dc), inc 1 st twice, 4 sc (UK dc) (12 sts).

Round 8: 1 sc (UK dc) into each st of previous round (12 sts).

Round 9: 5 sc (UK dc), inc 1 st twice, 5 sc (UK dc) (14 sts).

Round 10: 1 sc (UK dc) into each st of previous round (14 sts).

Round 11: dec 1 st, 4 sc (UK dc), inc 1 st twice, 4 sc (UK dc), dec 1 st (14 sts).

Secure the yarn and fasten off.

EYES (MAKE 2)

Using 2.5mm (B-1/UK 13) hook and Black yarn, work 6 sc (UK dc) into a magic ring. Join in a round with 1 sl st into the first st. Secure the yarn and fasten off.

FINISHING OFF

Use whip stitch to sew the top to the tummy. Stuff before sewing up. Sew the eyes to the head at rows 21 and 22. Using White yarn, embroider two French knots on each eye and two eyelashes in Black yarn. Use whip stitch to sew the tail lobes to the last six rows at the top of the whale's tail. The tail lobe increases should face the back.

Pierrot
THE FROG

This talented little frog paints and splashes just like the old masters. His works have already been displayed in Paris, London and New York. So naturally, if you're doing all that travelling, you need to have good shoes.

HEIGHT

★ Approx. 12½in (32cm)

MATERIAL

★ Lang Yarns Merino+ Color (100% merino wool); 1 ball of Green 0044 and small amounts of Red 0061; 100g/196yd/180m
★ Lana Grossa Cool Wool Big (100% merino wool); scraps of Black 627 and White 601; 50g/131yd/120m
★ 2.5mm (B-1/UK 13) crochet hook
★ Toy stuffing
★ Tapestry needle

HEAD

Work in spiral rounds. This means the rounds are not finished with a sl st, nor do you work a turning ch at the beg of a new round. Place marker at beg of round to make it easier to find.

Round 1: using Green yarn, work 13 ch, sc (UK dc) into second ch from hook, 1 sc (UK dc) into each of next 10 ch, 4 sc (UK dc) into last ch. Continue working on the other side of the length of ch: 10 sc (UK dc), 3 sc (UK dc) into first ch (28 sts).

Round 2: 12 sc (UK dc), inc 1 st twice, 12 sc (UK dc), inc 1 st twice (32 sts).

Round 3: inc 1 st, 10 sc (UK dc), inc 1 st, 1 sc (UK dc), inc 1 st twice, 1 sc (UK dc), inc 1 st, 10 sc (UK dc), inc 1 st, 1 sc (UK dc), inc 1 st twice, 1 sc (UK dc) (40 sts).

Round 4: 1 sc (UK dc), inc 1 st, 10 sc (UK dc), inc 1 st, 27 sc (UK dc) (42 sts).

Round 5: 2 sc (UK dc), inc 1 st, 10 sc (UK dc), inc 1 st, 2 sc (UK dc), inc 1 st, 24 sc (UK dc), inc 1 st (46 sts).

Round 6: 1 sc (UK dc) into each st of previous round (46 sts).

Round 7: 3 sc (UK dc), inc 1 st, 10 sc (UK dc), inc 1 st, 31 sc (UK dc) (48 sts).

Rounds 8–17: 1 sc (UK dc) into each st of previous round (48 sts).

Round 18: *7 sc (UK dc), skip 1 st*, rep from * to * five more times (42 sts).

Round 19: 3 sc (UK dc), skip 1 st, *6 sc (UK dc), skip 1 st*, rep from * to * four more times, 3 sc (UK dc) (36 sts).

Round 20: *5 sc (UK dc), skip 1 st*, rep from * to * five more times (30 sts). Stuff the head.

Round 21: *4 sc (UK dc), skip 1 st*, rep from * to * five more times (24 sls).

Round 22: *3 sc (UK dc), skip 1 st*, rep from * to * five more times (18 sts).

Round 23: *2 sc (UK dc), skip 1 st*, rep from * to * five more times (12 sts).

Round 24: *1 sc (UK dc), skip 1 st*, rep from * to * five more times (6 sts).

Round 25: *skip 1 st, 1 sl st*, rep from * to * twice more (3 sts).

Secure yarn and fasten off.

BODY

Work in spiral rounds. This means the rounds are not finished with a sl st, nor do you work a turning ch at the beg of a new round.

Round 1: using Green yarn, work 6 sc (UK dc) into a magic ring (6 sts).

Round 2: inc 1 st six times (12 sts).

Round 3: *1 sc (UK dc), inc 1 st*, rep from * to * five more times (18 sts).

Round 4: *2 sc (UK dc), inc 1 st*, rep from * to * five more times (24 sts).

Round 5: *3 sc (UK dc), inc 1 st*, rep from * to * five more times (30 sts).

Round 6: *4 sc (UK dc), inc 1 st*, rep from * to * five more times (36 sts).

Round 7: *5 sc (UK dc), inc 1 st*, rep from * to * five more times (42 sts).

Round 8: *6 sc (UK dc), inc 1 st*, rep from * to * five more times (48 sts).

Round 9: *7 sc (UK dc), inc 1 st*, rep from * to * five more times (54 sts).

Round 10: *8 sc (UK dc), inc 1 st*, rep from * to * five more times (60 sts).

Round 11: 1 sc (UK dc) into each st of previous round (60 sts).

Round 12: *9 sc (UK dc), inc 1 st*, rep from * to * five more times (66 sts).

Rounds 13–16: 1 sc (UK dc) into each st of previous round (66 sts).

Round 17: *10 sc (UK dc), skip 1 st*, rep from * to * five more times (60 sts).

Round 18: 1 sc (UK dc) into each st of previous round (60 sts).

Round 19: *9 sc (UK dc), miss 1 st*, rep from * to * five more times (54 sts).

Round 20: 1 sc (UK dc) into each st of previous round (54 sts).

Round 21: *8 sc (UK dc), skip 1 st*, rep from * to * five more times (48 sts).

Round 22: 1 sc (UK dc) into each st of previous round (48 sts).

Round 23: *7 sc (UK dc) skip 1 st*, rep from * to * five more times (42 sts).

Round 24: 1 sc (UK dc) into each st of previous round (42 sts).

Round 25: *6 sc (UK dc), skip 1 st*, rep from * to * five more times (36 sts).

Round 26: 1 sc (UK dc) into each st of previous round (36 sts).

Round 27: *5 sc (UK dc), skip 1 st*, rep from * to * five more times (30 sts).

Rounds 28–33: 1 sc (UK dc) into each st of previous round (30 sts).

Secure the yarn and fasten off. Stuff the body.

ARMS (MAKE 2)
FINGERS

Work in rounds. At the end of each round, work 1 sl st into first st in round, 1 ch and turn.

Round 1: using Green yarn, work 6 sc (UK dc) into a magic ring (6 sts).

Round 2: *1 sc (UK dc), inc 1 st*, rep from * to * twice more (9 sts).

Round 3: 1 sc (UK dc) into each st of previous round (9 sts).

Round 4: *1 sc (UK dc), dec 1 st*, rep from * to * twice more (6 sts).

Rounds 5–8: 1 sc (UK dc) into each st of previous round (6 sts).

Secure the yarn and fasten off. Now work two more fingers. Do not fasten off yarn after the third finger (called 'first finger' below), but continue crocheting as follows:

Round 9: 3 sc (UK dc) in the first finger, 3 sc (UK dc) in the second finger, 6 sc (UK dc) in the last finger, 3 sc (UK dc) in the second finger, 3 sc (UK dc) in the first finger (18 sts).

Rounds 10–14: 1 sc (UK dc) into each st of previous round (18 sts).

Stuff the fingers and hand.

Round 15: dec 1 st nine times (9 sts).

Rounds 16–32: 1 sc (UK dc) into each st of previous round (9 sts).

Secure the yarn and fasten off. Stuff the arm, making sure that you only stuff the upper part loosely.

LEGS (MAKE 2)

Start off working in rounds. At the end of each round, work 1 sl st into first st in round, 1 ch and turn.

Round 1: using Red yarn, work 7 ch, 1 sc (UK dc) into second ch from hook, 1 sc (UK dc) into next 4 ch, 4 sc (UK dc) into last ch. Continue working on the other side of the length of ch: 4 sc (UK dc), 3 sc (UK dc) into first ch (16 sts).

Round 2: 6 sc (UK dc), inc 1 st twice, 7 sc (UK dc), inc 1 st (19 sts).

Round 3: 6 sc (UK dc), 2 hdc (UK htr) in 1 st twice, 7 sc (UK dc), inc 1 st twice (25 sts).

Round 4: work into the back bar of the stitch only: 1 sc (UK dc) into each st of previous round (25 sts).

Round 5: 4 sc (UK dc), dec 1 st six times, 9 sc (UK dc) (19 sts).

Round 6: 1 sc (UK dc) into each st of previous round (19 sts).

Round 7: 3 sc (UK dc), dec 1 st four times, 8 sc (UK dc) (15 sts).

Rounds 8 and 9: 1 sc (UK dc) into each st of previous round (15 sts).

Round 10: work into the front bar of the stitch only: *inc 1 st, 1 sc (UK dc)*, rep from * to * six more times, inc 1 st (23 sts).

Secure the yarn and fasten off. Stuff the foot. Join Green yarn to the back bar of the first st in round 9, and continue working in spiral rounds as follows:

Round 10: *3 sc (UK dc), dec 1 st*, rep from * to * twice more (12 sts).

Rounds 11–25: 1 sc (UK dc) into each st of previous round (12 sts).

Round 26: 3 sc (UK dc), dec 1 st, 7 sc (UK dc) (11 sts).

Round 27: 1 sc (UK dc) into each st of previous round (11 sts).

Round 28: 6 sc (UK dc), dec 1 st, 3 sc (UK dc) (10 sts).

Rounds 29 and 30: 1 sc (UK dc) into each st of previous round (10 sts).

Secure the yarn and fasten off. Stuff three-quarters of the leg.

EYES (MAKE 2)

Work in spiral rounds. This means the rounds are not finished with a sl st, nor do you work a turning ch at the beg of a new round.

Round 1: using Green yarn, work 5 sc (UK dc) into a magic ring (5 sts).

Round 2: inc 1 st five times (10 st).

Round 3: 4 sc (UK dc), inc 1 st, 4 sc (UK dc), inc 1 st (12 sts).

Round 4: 1 sc (UK dc) into each st of previous round (12 sts).

Round 5: *3 sc (UK dc), inc 1 st*, rep from * to * twice more (15 sts).

Round 6: *4 sc (UK dc), inc 1 st*, rep from * to * twice more (18 sts).

Round 7: *2 sc (UK dc), inc 1 st*, rep from * to * five more times (24 sts).

Secure the yarn and fasten off. Stuff the eye.

WHITES OF THE EYES (MAKE 2)

Work in rounds. At the end of each round, work 1 sl st into first st in round, 1 ch and turn.

Round 1: using White yarn, work 1 sc (UK dc), 1 dc (UK tr), 2 sc (UK dc), 1 dc (UK tr), 1 sc (UK dc) into a magic ring (6 sts).

Round 2: 2 sc (UK dc) in 1 st, 3 dc (UK tr) in 1 st, 2 sc (UK dc) in 1 st twice, 3 dc (UK tr) in 1 st, 2 sc (UK dc) in 1 st (14 sts).

Secure the yarn and fasten off.

PUPILS (MAKE 2)

Round 1: using Black yarn, work 6 sc (UK dc) into a magic ring (6 sts).

Join in a round with 1 sl st into the first st. Secure the yarn and fasten off.

FINISHING OFF

Hold the head so the two increases in round 4 are facing upwards. This is the top of the head. Use whip stitch to sew the last round of the eyes to rounds 12–18 of the head. Backstitch along the last round of the white of the eye to attach it to the head. Use backstitch to sew a pupil to the bottom of the white of the eye. Using White yarn, embroider two French knots to the pupils. Use whip stitch to sew the last round of the body to the underside of the head. Press the last round of each arm together, and use whip stitch to sew the edges to round 33 of the body. Press the last rounds of the legs together and sew the edges to round 9 of the body.

Charlie
THE TURTLE

Charlie is a talented singer – well, he thinks so, anyway. His audience is slightly more reserved, but that doesn't prevent him from sitting on his stone and belting out the oddest ballads at the top of his lungs.

LENGTH
★ Approx. 12½in (32cm)

MATERIALS
★ Lang Yarns Merino 70 (98% merino wool, 2% polyester); 1 ball of Camel 0039; 50g/76yd/70m
★ Lang Yarns Merino 70 Dégradé (98% merino wool, 2% polyester); 1 ball of Beige/Mixed 0075; 100g/153yd/140mg
★ Austermann Merino 160 (100% merino wool); scraps of Black 202 and White 201; 50g/174yd/160m
★ 4mm (G-6/UK 8) and 2.5mm (B-1/UK 13) crochet hooks
★ Toy stuffing
★ Tapestry needle

HEAD
Work in spiral rounds. This means the rounds are not finished with a sl st, nor do you work a turning ch at the beg of a new round.

Round 1: using 4mm (G-6/UK 8) hook and Camel yarn, work 6 sc (UK dc) into a magic ring (6 sts).
Round 2: inc 1 st six times (12 sts).
Round 3: *1 sc (UK dc), inc 1 st*, rep from * to * five more times (18 sts).
Round 4: *2 sc (UK dc), inc 1 st*, rep from * to * five more times (24 sts).
Round 5: *3 sc (UK dc), inc 1 st*, rep from * to * five more times (30 sts).
Round 6: *4 sc (UK dc), inc 1 st*, rep from * to * five more times (36 sts).
Round 7: *5 sc (UK dc), inc 1 st*, rep from * to * five more times (42 sts).
Rounds 8–14: 1 sc (UK dc) into each st of previous round (42 sts).
Round 15: *5 sc (UK dc), dec 1 st*, rep from * to * five more times (36 sts).
Round 16: *4 sc (UK dc), dec 1 st*, rep from * to * five more times (30 sts).

Round 17: *3 sc (UK dc), dec 1 st*, rep from * to * five more times (24 sts).
Rounds 18–23: 1 sc (UK dc) into each st of previous round (24 sts).
Secure the yarn and fasten off. Stuff the head.

SHELL
The shell is made up of a total of seven hexagons. The following instructions explain how to make a hexagon. Work in spiral rounds. This means the rounds are not finished with a sl st, nor do you work a turning ch at the beg of a new round.

Round 1: using 4mm (G-6/UK 8) hook and Beige/Mixed yarn, work 6 sc (UK dc) into a magic ring (6 sts).
Round 2: inc 1 st six times (12 sts).
Round 3: *1 sc (UK dc), inc 1 st*, rep from * to * five more times (18 sts).
Round 4: *2 sc (UK dc), inc 1 st*, rep from * to * five more times (24 sts).

Round 5: *3 sc (UK dc), inc 1 st*, rep from * to * five more times (30 sts).
Round 6: *4 sc (UK dc), inc 1 st*, rep from * to * five more times (36 sts).
Round 7: *5 sc (UK dc), inc 1 st*, rep from * to * five more times (42 sts).
Round 8: *6 sc (UK dc), inc 1 st*, rep from * to * five more times (48 sts).
Secure the yarn and fasten off.
Choose one of the hexagons as the middle one and use mattress stitch to sew the other hexagons to the sides of this one. Then sew the sides of the neighbouring hexagons together with mattress stitch to make a kind of bowl. This is the shell.

TUMMY
To make the tummy, join Camel yarn to the back bar of any st in the shell opening, and work around it in spiral rounds. This means the rounds are not finished with 1 sl st, nor do you work a turning ch at the beg of a new round.

Round 1: using 4mm (G-6/UK 8) hook and Camel yarn, work into the back bar of the stitch only: 1 sc (UK dc) into each st of previous round (48 sts).
Round 2: 1 sc (UK dc) into each st of previous round (48 sts).
Round 3: *6 sc (UK dc), dec 1 st*, rep from * to * five more times (42 sts).
Round 4: *5 sc (UK dc), dec 1 st*, rep from * to * five more times (36 sts).
Stuff the shell.
Round 5: *4 sc (UK dc), dec 1 st*, rep from * to * five more times (30 sts).
Round 6: *3 sc (UK dc), dec 1 st*, rep from * to * five more times (24 sts).
Round 7: *2 sc (UK dc), dec 1 st*, rep from * to * five more times (18 sts).
Round 8: *1 sc (UK dc), dec 1 st*, rep from * to * five more times (12 sts).
Round 9: dec 1 st six times (6 sts).
Round 10: *skip 1 st, 1 sl st*, rep from * to * twice more (3 sts).
Secure the yarn and fasten off.

LEGS (MAKE 2)

Work in spiral rounds. This means the rounds are not finished with a sl st, nor do you work a turning ch at the beg of a new round.

Round 1: using 4mm (G-6/UK 8) hook and Camel yarn, work 6 sc (UK dc) into a magic ring (6 sts).

Round 2: inc 1 st six times (12 sts).

Round 3: *1 sc (UK dc), inc 1 st*, rep from * to * five more times (18 sts).

Round 4: *2 sc (UK dc), inc 1 st*, rep from * to * five more times (24 sts).

Round 5: work into the back bar of the stitch only: 1 sc (UK dc) into each st of previous round (24 sts).

Rounds 6 and 7: 1 sc (UK dc) into each st of previous round (24 sts).

Round 8: 6 sc (UK dc), dec 1 st six times, 6 sc (UK dc) (18 sts).

Rounds 9–18: 1 sc (UK dc) in each st of the previous round (18 sts).

Secure the yarn and fasten off. Stuff the leg three-quarters full.

ARMS (MAKE 2)

Work in spiral rounds. This means the rounds are not finished with a sl st, nor do you work a turning ch at the beg of a new round.

Round 1: using 4mm (G-6/UK 8) hook and Camel yarn, work 6 sc (UK dc) into a magic ring (6 sts).

Round 2: inc 1 st six times (12 sts).

Rounds 3–7: 1 sc (UK dc) into each st of previous round (12 sts).

Round 8: *4 sc (UK dc), dec 1 st*, rep from * to * once more (10 sts).

Rounds 9–13: 1 sc (UK dc) into each st of previous round (10 sts).

Secure yarn and fasten off. Stuff the arm three-quarters full.

EYES (MAKE 2)

Round 1: using 2.5mm (B-1/UK 13) hook and Black yarn, work 6 sc (UK dc) into a magic ring (6 sts). Join with sl st to first st to make a ring.

Secure the yarn and fasten off.

FINISHING OFF

Use mattress stitch to sew the last round of the head to the middle of the edge of one of the outer shell hexagons. Press the last round of an arm together, and use whip stitch to sew the edge to the tummy, below the head at rounds 1–3. Press the last round of a leg together, and use whip stitch to sew the edge to the opposite side of the arms at the first round of the tummy. Sew the eyes to the head. Using White yarn, embroider two French knots to the eyes. Sew two eyelashes next to each eye with Black yarn.

Charlotte
THE OCTOPUS

Let's Go

HEIGHT
★ Approx. 11¾in (30cm)

MATERIALS
★ Austermann Merino 160 (100% merino wool); 2 balls of Azur 222, 1 ball of Petrol 233 and scraps of Black 202, White 201, Rosa 211 and Fuchsia 219; 50g/175yd/160m
★ 2.5mm (B-1/UK13) crochet hook
★ Toy stuffing
★ Tapestry needle

HEAD
Work in spiral rounds. This means the rounds are not finished with a sl st, nor do you work a turning ch at the beg of a new round.

Round 1: using Azur yarn, work 6 sc (UK dc) into a magic ring (6 sts).

Round 2: inc 1 st six times (12 sts).

Round 3: *1 sc (UK dc), inc 1 st*, rep from * to * five more times (18 sts).

Round 4: *2 sc (UK dc), inc 1 st*, rep from * to * five more times (24 sts).

Round 5: *3 sc (UK dc), inc 1 st*, rep from * to * five more times (30 sts).

Round 6: *4 sc (UK dc), inc 1 st*, rep from * to * five more times (36 sts).

Round 7: *5 sc (UK dc), inc 1 st*, rep from * to * five more times (42 sts).

Round 8: *6 sc (UK dc), inc 1 st*, rep from * to * five more times (48 sts).

Round 9: *7 sc (UK dc), inc 1 st*, rep from * to * five more times (54 sts).

Round 10: *8 sc (UK dc), inc 1 st*, rep from * to * five more times (60 sts).

Round 11: *9 sc (UK dc), inc 1 st*, rep from * to * five more times (66 sts).

Round 12: *10 sc (UK dc), inc 1 st*, rep from * to * five more times (72 sts).

Rounds 13–15: 1 sc (UK dc) into each st of previous round (72 sts).

Round 16: *11 sc (UK dc), inc 1 st*, rep from * to * five more times (78 sts).

Rounds 17–24: 1 sc (UK dc) into each st of previous round (78 sts).

Round 25: *11 sc (UK dc), dec 1 st*, rep from * to * five more times (72 sts).

Rounds 26 and 27: 1 sc (UK dc) into each st of previous round (72 sts).

Round 28: *10 sc (UK dc), dec 1 st*, rep from * to * five more times (66 sts).

Rounds 29 and 30: 1 sc (UK dc) into each st of previous round (66 sts).

Round 31: *9 sc (UK dc), dec 1 st*, rep from * to * five more times (60 sts).

Round 32: *8 sc (UK dc), dec 1 st*, rep from * to * five more times (54 sts).

Round 33: 1 sc (UK dc) into each st of previous round (54 sts).

Round 34: *7 sc (UK dc), dec 1 st*, rep from * to * five more times (48 sts).

Round 35: 24 sc (UK dc), *6 sc (UK dc), dec 1 st*, rep from * to * twice more (45 sts).

Round 36: 24 sc (UK dc), *5 sc (UK dc), dec 1 st*, rep from * to * twice more (42 sts).

Rounds 37–39: 1 sc (UK dc) into each st of previous round (42 sts).

Round 40: *6 sc (UK dc), inc 1 st*, rep from * to * five more times (48 sts).

Do not fasten off the yarn.

Continue working the tentacles in rows. At the end of each row, work 1 ch and turn the work.

Row 1: 6 sc (UK dc) (6 sts). Do not work the remaining sts.

Rows 2–18: 1 sc (UK dc) into each st of previous row (6 sts).

Row 19: 2 sc (UK dc), dec 1 st, 2 sc (UK dc) (5 sts).

Rows 20–37: 1 sc (UK dc) into each st of previous row (5 sts).

Row 38: dec 1 st, 1 sc (UK dc), dec 1 st (3 sts).

Rows 39–44: 1 sc (UK dc) into each st of previous round (3 sts).

Round 12: 1 sc (UK dc) into each st of previous round (48 sts).

Do not fasten off. Continue working the tentacles in rows. Work 1 ch at the end of each row and turn the work.

Row 1: 6 sc (UK dc) (6 sts). Do not work the remaining sts.

Rows 2–18: 1 sc (UK dc) into each st of previous row (6 sts).

Row 19: 2 sc (UK dc), dec 1 st, 2 sc (UK dc) (5 sts).

Rows 20–37: 1 sc (UK dc) into each st of previous row (5 sts).

Row 38: dec 1 st, 1 sc (UK dc), dec 1 st (3 sts).

Rows 39–44: 1 sc (UK dc) into each st of previous row (3 sts).

Row 45: skip 1 st, dec 1 st (1 st).

Join Petrol yarn to the first unworked st of round 12 and work rows 1–45 a total of eight times.

EYES (MAKE 2)

Round 1: using Black yarn, work 6 sc (UK dc) into a magic ring (6 sts).

Join in a round with 1 sl st into the first st. Secure the yarn and fasten off.

FINISHING OFF

Stuff the head. Place the tentacle underside with the right side facing outwards onto the body, lining up the tentacles. Hold the work so you are looking at the top of the head, and using Azur yarn, crochet the tentacles together along the edge with 1 round of sc (UK dc) in each st. Work 3 st into each st of the tip of a tentacle. As you are working, gradually stuff the tentacles. Sew the eyes to the lower part of the face. Using White yarn, embroider two French knots onto the eyes and two eyelashes with Black yarn. Using Rosa yarn, make a few backstitches a couple of lines below and slightly behind each eye for the cheeks. With Fuschia yarn, sew a small 'v' between the eyes for the mouth.

Row 45: skip 1 st, dec 1 st (1 st). Secure the yarn and fasten off.

Join the yarn to the first unworked st of round 40 and work rows 1–45 for the next tentacle. Repeat six times until you have eight tentacles.

TENTACLE UNDERSIDE

Work in spiral rounds. This means the rounds are not finished with a sl st, nor do you work a turning ch at the beg of a new round.

Round 1: using Petrol yarn, work 6 sc (UK dc) into a magic ring (6 sts).

Round 2: inc 1 st six times (12 sts).

Round 3: *1 sc (UK dc), inc 1 st*, rep from * to * five more times (18 sts).

Round 4: *2 sc (UK dc), inc 1 st*, rep from * to * five more times (24 sts).

Round 5: 1 sc (UK dc) into each st of previous round (24 sts).

Round 6: *3 sc (UK dc), inc 1 st*, rep from * to * five more times (30 sts).

Round 7: 1 sc (UK dc) into each st of previous round (30 sts).

Round 8: *4 sc (UK dc), inc 1 st*, rep from * to * five more times (36 sts).

Round 9: 1 sc (UK dc) into each st of previous round (36 sts).

Round 10: *5 sc (UK dc), inc 1 st*, rep from * to * five more times (42 sts).

Round 11: *6 sc (UK dc), inc 1 st*, rep from * to * five more times (48 sts).

First published in Great Britain 2018
by Search Press Limited
Wellwood, North Farm Road
Tunbridge Wells, Kent TN2 3DR

© Edition Michael Fischer GmbH, 2016
www.emf-verlag.de

This translation of Wollig-weiche Knuffeltiere häkeln first
published in Germany by Edition Michael Fischer GmbH in
2016 is published by arrangement with Silke Bruenink
Agency, Munich, Germany.

English Translation by Burravoe Translation Services

ISBN: 978-1-78221-577-6

If you have difficulty in obtaining any of the materials
and equipment mentioned in this book, then please visit
the Search Press website for details of suppliers:
www.searchpress.com

Printed in China through Asia Pacific Offset

Cover design: Silvia Keller
Illustrations: Patrick Wittmann, Munich
Product management: Anna Zwicklbauer
Layout: Silvia Keller & Michaela Zander
Illustrations: © alicedaniel/Shutterstock (p. 14; p. 15),
© andromina/Shutterstock (p. 3; p. 86; p. 88; p. 92; p. 96),
© anfisa focusova/Shutterstock (p. 126; p. 127),
© angkrit/Shutterstock (p. 96; p. 98),
© Bakai/Shutterstock (p. 3; p. 100; p. 102; p. 106; p. 110),
© Curly Roo/Shutterstock (p. 140; p. 142),
© daisybee/Shutterstock (p. 60; p. 62), © Emir Simsek/
Shutterstock (p. 128; p. 130), © gutsulyak/Shutterstock (p.
52; p. 55), © iDesign/Shutterstock (p. 136; p. 138),
© Kapreski/Shutterstock (p. 3; p. 64; p. 66; p. 70;
p. 74; p. 80), © KateChe/Shutterstock (p. 66; p. 69),
© KittyVektor/Shutterstock (p. 42; p. 45), © Kurdanfell/
Shutterstock (p. 3; p. 14; p. 16; p. 22; p. 26;
p. 30; p. 34; p. 126; p. 128; p. 132; p. 136; p. 140),
© LenLis/Shutterstock (p. 102; p. 105), © maglyvi/
Shutterstock (p. 22; p. 25), © Marish/Shutterstock (p. 64;
p. 65; p. 86; p. 87; p. 100; p. 101; p. 114; p. 115; p. 116;
p. 118),
© MilanM/Shutterstock (p. 132; p. 134; p. 135), © MSSA/
Shutterstock (p. 40; p. 41), © Nebojsa Konti/Shutterstock (p.
56; p. 58; p. 59), © Panptys/Shutterstock (p.3; p. 114;
p. 116; p. 120), © PureSolution/Shutterstock (p. 26; p. 29),
© Raura7/Shutterstock (p. 86; p. 87), © Robbie Bautista/
Shutterstock (p. 92), © serazetdinov/Shutterstock
(p. 106; p. 108), © winnievinzence/Shutterstock
(p. 120; p. 122), © Sanatchanan/Shutterstock (p. 123; p. 124),
© VectorEps/Shutterstock (p. 77; p. 78), © vectorstockstoker
(p. 34; p. 37), © Victor Metelskiy/Shutterstock (p. 74; p. 76;
p. 80; p. 82), © VoodooDot/Shutterstock (p. 3; p. 40; p. 42;
p. 46; p. 52; p. 56; p. 60), © Zakharchuk Nataliia/
Shutterstock (p. 140; p. 142)